A New Approach to Principal Preparation

Innovative Programs Share Their Practices and Lessons Learned

Acknowledgements

First and foremost, we want to thank Gretchen Rhines Cheney, our devoted writer who made sense of huge amounts of information from interviews, program materials and past drafts and, with incredible patience and persistence, created a strong product that allows other organizations to have a jump start in creating or revising their principal preparation programs. Saralyn Carrillo, Kelli Graham and Jeremy Smith, from the Rainwater Charitable Foundation organized us, arranged interviews, kept the larger RLA group on track and generally provided critical advice and feedback—thanks to them.

The Rainwater Leadership Alliance (RLA) as a group is responsible for the existence of this document. The teamwork and willingness to share work that all of the programs have shown throughout this project, as well as in the RLA gatherings, is tremendous and is a great example of adults in education working together to share what they have learned to move our country to be a place where all students can attend schools with strong leaders and excellent teaching and learning. The Advisory Committee members, (generally the leaders of their organizations and often lead contributors, in italics below) guided this project and involved their organizations, as well as each person who worked on a content area small group and contributed tremendously by sharing examples, reading drafts, chasing down information and generally being incredible at responding to what always seemed like time sensitive needs. This incredible teamwork is an illustration of what is possible when educators work together across different organizations. Thanks to them for their willingness, openness with their work and their responsiveness and dedication. Specifically, those who contributed are:

Gwinnett County Public Schools: *Glenn Pethel*, Frances Davis, Linda Daniels, and Kendra Washington-Bass
KIPP: *Kelly Wright*, Jack Carey, Lara Knight, Terence Johnson, and Sehba Ali

New Leaders for New Schools: *Jon Schnur, LaVerne Srinivasan*, Ben Fenton, Drema Brown, Helen Dixon, Mark Murphy, Mike Moore, Rika Wilcox, Ronald Rapatalo, Stephanie Fitzgerald, Tonieh Schmitz, and Darlene Merry
NYC Leadership Academy: *Sandra Stein*, Kathy Nadurak, Courtney Welsh, Holly Carmichael, and Ilene Friedman
RICE University's Education Entrepreneurship Program: *Andrea Hodge* and Colleen Dippel
University of Illinois at Chicago: *Steve Tozer*, Peter Martinez, and Shelby Cosner
The University of Virginia's Darden/Curry Partnership for Leaders in Education: *LeAnn Buntrock* and Dennis Woodruff
The New School: *Karen DeMoss*
School Leaders Network: *Elizabeth Neale* and Jody Roy
Education Pioneers: *Frances McLaughlin*
Long Beach Unified School District: *Kristi Kahl*
Teach For America: *Heather Anichini*
University of Chicago: *Tim Knowles*
University of Pennsylvania: *Doug Lynch* and Mike Johanek
Principals: Tatiana Epanchin and Michelle Pierre-Farid

We could not have done this project without the generous financial backing of the Rainwater Charitable Foundation, which funded and led all of the Rainwater Leadership Alliance convenings that inspired this work, and funded the dedicated time over the course of several months for us to pull mountains of information together into a coherent document. We also thank The Eli and Edythe Broad Foundation for all of their work in the area of principal preparation, as well as their early thought leadership and financial support that helped many of the RLA programs develop, as well as the significant early work researching, gathering information and preparing drafts for this document, specifically by Christine DeLeon and Alyssa Simon with guidance from Frances McLaughlin, Luis de la Fuente, and Dan Katzir. Thanks also go to the Wallace Foundation, particularly Richard Laine, and Jody Spiro for thought partnership as we initially launched this project.

Table of Contents

5   Letter from The Rainwater Charitable Foundation

7   The Rainwater Leadership Alliance

8   Introduction

12   How to Read This Document

14   **Chapter 1:** Competency Framework

20   **Chapter 2:** Building a Candidate Pool

42   **Chapter 3:** Selecting Candidates

64   **Chapter 4:** Training and Developing Fellows

92   **Chapter 5:** Supporting Principals

116   **Chapter 6:** Program Evaluation

128   Conclusion

130   Rainwater Leadership Alliance Program Summaries

140   Appendices

142   **Appendix A:** Introduction

146   **Appendix B:** Competency Framework

157   **Appendix C:** Building a Candidate Pool

159   **Appendix D:** Selecting Candidates

172   **Appendix E:** Training and Developing Fellows

194   **Appendix F:** Supporting Principals

Letter from the Rainwater Charitable Foundation

Kelly Garrett, Executive Director

It is with great enthusiasm that we offer this document, *A New Approach to Principal Preparation*, to share the practices of the programs that make up the Rainwater Leadership Alliance with the education community. It is our belief that school leadership is an essential lever for affecting student achievement and for ensuring that all children have access to the highest-quality education. The evidence is clear that quality teaching is critical. However, to achieve teacher effectiveness <u>at scale</u>, schools need effective principals who create a school culture of high expectations, focused on learning, for both students and adults. Schools must become the kinds of places where teachers can learn in practice how to meet the needs of their students and work together to serve all students. The key to strengthening teaching is outstanding leadership in every school.

According to a 2004 report, *How Leadership Influences Student Learning*, funded by the Wallace Foundation, "There are virtually no documented instances of troubled schools being turned around in the absence of intervention by talented leaders. While other factors within the school also contribute to such turnarounds, leadership is the catalyst."[1] *It is the combination of highly effective teaching with highly capable school leadership that will change outcomes for children in our schools—not one or the other but both.*

At the Rainwater Charitable Foundation (RCF), our benefactor, Richard Rainwater, believes strongly that schools, like any other organization, must have effective leadership to be successful. Therefore in 2005, he asked the Foundation team to explore the most ground-breaking leadership training and preparation programs in the country and to learn from them in order to better invest in principal training and development to meet the needs of our nation's toughest and neediest schools.

The RCF team established a theory about what constitutes a successful leadership training program based on effective practices in education and other sectors. Programs must aggressively recruit candidates and be highly selective about which candidates are ready for leadership. They must then carefully train their aspiring leaders, and part of that training must be hands-on experience. Finally, programs have to hold themselves and their alumni accountable for the impact they have on the bottom line: in this case, student achievement.

Our search for programs that hold to these tenets resulted in the formation of the Rainwater Leadership Alliance (RLA). The RLA entrepreneurs approach the work differently than traditional principal preparation programs in that they actively recruit talent, are very selective in admissions, emphasize practice-based training, and engage closely with the districts and schools where their graduates are ultimately placed. Perhaps most importantly, the RLA programs see it as their obligation to prepare leaders who can dramatically improve student achievement and sustain that improvement over time. While many of these programs are still relatively new, they all at least have some evidence indicating that they are effectively preparing principals for success in the complex and high-stress environment of schools today. And because they track this data, they can make real-time changes to their model in order to get to higher student outcomes. Some of the more mature programs in the RLA have engaged external evaluators and are showing positive results.

Over the past three years, RLA members have been convening on a regular basis to share approaches, discuss their work, and collectively improve programming and outcomes. Other providers and training programs from districts, states, nonprofits, and universities have expressed great interest in these conversations. The RCF has therefore decided to capture and share the experiences of the RLA members and the lessons they have learned along the way from their work in low-income, high-need, mainly urban schools.

This document is written with the full understanding that, while early results show promise, none of the RLA members have perfected the principal training model. But their collective experiences have generated a great deal of information that can deeply benefit the field. In some cases, the approaches presented may appear to run counter to prevailing practice. It is our hope that by capturing and sharing the evolving thinking of these innovative program architects, we can help other programs gain traction more quickly, producing school leaders who deliver the highest student outcomes—at even greater scale.

The job of school principal may be one of the toughest in our nation—and one of the most valuable. High-quality school leaders are in great demand and there are strong calls for principal preparation programs to meet the need more effectively. If we want to turn around our schools and improve student achievement for all children year after year, we must address this leadership challenge.

It is our hope that this document will be informative in assisting programs in improving their own practices and in producing a new generation of school principals who are ready to tackle the challenging and rewarding work of improving and running our nation's neediest schools. Effective leaders are essential to accelerating and increasing student achievement.

Sincerely,

Kelly Garrett
Executive Director
The Rainwater Charitable Foundation

Rainwater Leadership Alliance

The Rainwater Leadership Alliance, founded by the Rainwater Charitable Foundation and The Eli and Edythe Broad Foundation, is a coalition committed to improving the quality of school leadership in our public schools to ensure that all children achieve at high academic levels and are prepared to succeed in life.

Founded in 2008, the Rainwater Leadership Alliance (RLA) is an action tank. Participating programs include school districts, universities, foundations, and nonprofits dedicated to amplifying the importance of quality school leadership as the critical enabler of academic growth and performance for children. They lead, manage, and support high-impact principal preparation and development programs (urban, rural, and suburban) operating in many regions of the country. The RLA exists to share data, provide exemplars, and promote and scale effective methods to develop and support PK-12 school leaders.

The RLA members represent not just one model, but several different approaches to high-quality principal preparation and development. They have various configurations and contexts of work environments, which influence how they structure their programs. What makes these school leader preparation programs unique is that they are committed to tracking data on their graduates and continually improving their models to ensure that every graduate is driving dramatic student achievement in schools, especially in low-income communities. The selected RLA members that are highlighted in some detail throughout this guide are listed in the chart below. Short summaries on their program models can be found at the end of this document.

DISTRICT-BASED	UNIVERSITY-BASED	NONPROFIT PROVIDERS
Gwinnett County Public Schools' Quality-Plus Leader Academy	Rice University's Education Entrepreneurship Program	Knowledge Is Power Program (KIPP) School Leadership Program
Long Beach Unified School District	The University of Illinois at Chicago	New Leaders for New Schools
	The University of Virginia's Darden/Curry Partnership for Leaders in Education	NYC Leadership Academy's Aspiring Principals Program
		School Leaders Network

The RLA also has other members including Education Pioneers, The New School's Institute for Urban Education, Teach For America, the University of Chicago Urban Education Institute, and the University of Pennsylvania.

Introduction

To dramatically improve our nation's public schools, we must focus on the essential role of school leaders. While teacher quality is the single biggest factor influencing student achievement, strong principals are key to teacher development and retention. In fact, principals account for 25 percent—and teachers 33 percent—of a school's total impact on achievement.[2]

Put simply, the principal is the best-positioned person in every school to ensure successive years of quality teaching for each child. Exemplary principals establish a climate that values effective teaching and ensures that the most promising teachers are selected, all teachers are developed and recognized, and those teachers who are not doing well by children are released. **It is the combination of highly effective teaching with highly capable school leadership that will change outcomes for children in our schools—not one or the other but both**.

In order to ensure that our schools are led by effective principals, the field of principal preparation needs to be much more systematic and rigorous. A 2006 study by Columbia University's Teachers College President, Arthur Levine, concluded that the quality of most preparation programs for principals, superintendents and other education leaders was "very disappointing," especially at a time when high-quality educational leadership is critically needed for schools across the country.[3]

Traditionally, the processes and standards by which many principal preparation programs screen, select, and graduate candidates often lack rigor and do not adequately equip principals for the multi-faceted role of effective instructional leader. Too many of them admit students based on educational background information alone, without probing for important qualities such as resiliency, results orientation, belief in all children's ability to learn, commitment, and integrity required to do the job well. Once enrolled, the focus is often on earning a credential through a series of courses without having deep school-based experiences that allow students to practice, make mistakes, and learn firsthand what it takes to run a school. And, most programs do not provide the kinds of transitional supports needed to ensure that their newly minted principals succeed and stay on the job. Finally, most programs do not hold themselves accountable for the on-the-job performance of their graduates.

Lessons from the Rainwater Leadership Alliance

The RLA represents a portfolio of promising principal preparation programs that are on the forefront of innovation, exploring a new path forward. What sets apart these programs is that they are organized for the express purpose of preparing leaders who can dramatically improve student learning and close the achievement gap. Most are focused on urban schools and improving the achievement of underserved students, but some serve a broader population.

> "It is the combination of highly effective teaching with highly capable school leadership that will change outcomes for children in our schools—not one or the other but both."

SEE PAGE 7

Learn more about the Rainwater Leadership Alliance.

While many of the programs are still nascent, early results are promising. Three of the RLA programs have positive evidence of student achievement as documented by third-party evaluators. For example, RAND Corporation's multi-year longitudinal study of New Leaders for New Schools found that students in elementary and middle schools led for at least three years by New Leaders for New Schools principals are academically outpacing their peers by statistically significant margins (Martorell, Heaton, Gates, and Hamilton, 2010).[4] In the case of the Knowledge Is Power Program (KIPP), in a June 2010 report, Mathematica found that "for the vast majority of KIPP schools studied, impacts on students' state assessment scores in mathematics and reading are positive, statistically significant, and educationally substantial. Estimated impacts are frequently large enough to substantially reduce race- and income-based achievement gaps within three years of entering KIPP."[5] Finally, a study conducted by New York University's Institute for Education and Social Policy found that elementary and middle schools led by NYC Leadership Academy's Aspiring Principals Program graduates made greater gains in English Language Arts (ELA) than comparison schools, improving apace with city wide gains in ELA performance.[6]

The RLA is a coalition of innovative programs that share practices and distill lessons learned about improving principal effectiveness. Over the course of three years, the coalition members have come together to share data, provide exemplars, and promote and scale successful methods to develop and support school leaders. This document is the result of those conversations. Its purpose is to **provide a vision for making principal preparation programs more systematic and rigorous than the status quo**. While not a how-to guide, this document is intended as a reference manual, providing some in-depth examples about how and why specific program components came to be.

As you will see, **almost out of necessity, the RLA programs vary in their design specifics and approaches to implementation**. No program has unlimited resources and program architects are constantly evaluating the best way to use scarce funds and staff time to accomplish their ultimate mission: graduating principals who have the ability and stamina to produce lasting change in our nation's schools. The circumstances and contexts in which they work also drive programs to make different decisions about program design.

However, the RLA members share many common beliefs and principles, the most important of which is that they see students as their clients. They hold themselves accountable for improving student achievement outcomes and they track their graduates' performance as school leaders to ensure they are producing results.

The RLA programs share many similar design elements:
1. RLA programs start by defining a Competency Framework—the *set of skills, knowledge, and dispositions* that a principal must have in order to drive high levels of student achievement for all children. This set of standards uses the school as the lens to identify the most

important things high-performing principals must know and be able to do. The program then takes responsibility for finding candidates who can master these competencies and preparing them to be effective school leaders.

2. RLA programs rely on *strategic, proactive, and targeted recruiting strategies* to ensure that they have strong candidate pools and pipeline programs from which they can select candidates most likely to thrive in the program and grow into effective principals.

3. RLA programs are *highly selective and establish clear criteria and rigorous processes* to evaluate applicants' disposition, skills and knowledge. RLA programs require candidates to demonstrate their skills and dispositions through experiential events to evaluate whether candidates' behaviors and actions match their stated beliefs.

4. RLA programs believe that *training and development need to be experiential, giving trainees authentic opportunities to lead adults, make mistakes, and grow.* The development sequences are intentionally coordinated and integrated and include coursework; school-based residencies that take into account trainees' strengths and weaknesses; meaningful assessments; and ongoing coaching and feedback.

5. RLA programs believe that *ongoing support for graduates* to help them transition and grow on the job is important. RLA programs are clear that their interest is not only serving the individual, but supporting the leader to drive change school-wide to improve student achievement results.

6. RLA programs are committed to the notion of *continuous improvement and using data to assess the effectiveness of their principals and their programs.* Several of the programs have engaged third-party evaluators to help them examine their results and all of the members are collecting data to better understand how to make their programs more effective in preparing strong principals on behalf of students.

This document attempts to capture what these RLA programs are doing in each of these critical areas, the key lessons they have learned, and why they engage in the important work of preparing leaders for our nation's public schools. Throughout, we highlight the commonalities of the RLA programs, as well as provide some in-depth examples of the various approaches to specific program components. While many of the RLA programs are still emerging, they have already amassed significant learning from analyses of their results data that impacts all phases of their work. Our goal is to help principal preparation program architects—including districts, states, institutions of higher education, and nonprofits—learn from the collective work and thinking of the RLA members.

Our Challenge: Success at Scale

The intensity of this work cannot be underestimated. **If there is one message that resonates with all of the RLA members it is that principal preparation is hard work.** Leaders are difficult to find in any field. But the school principalship takes a particular person who can be an effective leader in the context of today's neediest schools.

The RLA programs invest significant resources of time, staff, and money in their quest to increase the number of successful principals. High-quality principal training is an expensive proposition. While the costs vary by program, some RLA members may spend up to $100,000 per program participant (not including the cost of residency salaries). To do this work at scale requires a commitment of resources.

It also requires the involvement of other stakeholders. The reality is that program design and implementation are only part of the equation. All principal preparation programs—whether they are third-party organizations, part of a higher education institution, or based in a district itself—serve districts and charter management organizations (CMOs) where schools are housed. Districts and states play a major role in establishing the operating conditions in which a principal works. The policies, practices, and overall infrastructure of these organizations have a large impact on a principal's ability to do the job effectively. Issues range from a principal's autonomy regarding staffing within the school, to incentives for individuals and schools that demonstrate success, to the organization of staffing supports and resources within the district, to the availability of high-quality student data reports.

In response to these challenges, some RLA programs have made it part of their mission to improve district and state conditions. Some have chosen to directly engage with districts and states to establish an environment where principals can gain traction on behalf of their schools.

The Purpose of This Document

While this document is primarily aimed at program architects and operators who are launching and designing new programs or revising and strengthening existing programs, it can also inform conversations at the state and district policy level. This is particularly relevant considering the U.S. Department of Education's current focus on strengthening the outcomes of principal preparation programs. If we are to do this work at scale, we must devise systemic approaches to prepare, place, and retain high-quality principals.

There is such urgency to this work. This document is intended to generate new thinking and help provide a more nuanced understanding of what it takes to prepare and support these critical leaders.

How to Read This Document

This document is organized around each of the important areas on the principal preparation continuum on the facing page. The chapters provide an in-depth look, beginning with the *Competency Framework* that undergirds all of the work, to the specifics of *building a candidate pool, selecting candidates, training and developing fellows,* and *supporting principals* post-graduation. The importance of *program evaluation* is stressed throughout and the final chapter addresses the topic specifically. The risk in presenting these as individual topics is that you, as the reader, might get the impression that these can be thought of separately. RLA members caution that this is not the case. **The entire continuum must be cohesive, as all of the components are interrelated and undergirded by the Principal Competency Framework.**

Given that leadership itself is not a manual of right and wrong answers, but rather a series of choices and a process of careful, deliberate decision-making, it is fitting that this document on preparing leaders is not prescriptive, but instead offers a variety of program approaches and examples, highlighting where RLA programs have shared values and principles. **The purpose of this document is to guide conversations among program architects, not to provide a replicable program model.**

In the four main chapters addressing the continuum components we present broad, overarching **Guiding Questions** at the beginning, as well as **Key Questions**, which are more targeted and specific for the subsections. Both are designed to help with decisions required in program design and implementation. While some program materials, tools and resources are included in the Appendices, there is no comprehensive checklist, no "plug and play" solution. Finally, the "Cost and Resource Allocation Considerations" section of each chapter is intentionally conceptual, outlining things to consider as you project your costs instead of trying to capture exact costs as programs vary widely.

CONTINUUM OF PRINCIPAL PREPARATION

CHAPTER 1
RLA programs start by defining a Competency Framework—the set of skills, knowledge and dispositions that a principal must have, in their context, in order to lead a school effectively to drive high levels of student achievement for all children.

CHAPTER 2
RLA programs rely on strategic, proactive and targeted recruiting strategies to ensure that they have strong candidate pools and pipeline programs from which they can select candidates most likely to thrive in the program and grow into effective principals.

CHAPTER 3
RLA programs are highly selective and establish clear criteria and rigorous processes to evaluate applicants. Their commitment to finding talented and passionate people who can ensure all children are learning in their schools drives every element of their selection process.

CHAPTER 4
RLA programs combine individual learning plans, explicit goals and delivery models, and coursework and experiential in-school practice with the power of peers within the program to help fellows stay on a steep learning curve and create a culture of continuous improvement.

CHAPTER 5
RLA programs support their new graduates by helping them identify and secure job placements in schools with needs that best match up with their strengths. They also provide on-going support to graduates in the form of professional development and ongoing coaching to help them grow on the job.

| DEVELOP A PRINCIPAL COMPETENCY FRAMEWORK | BUILD A CANDIDATE POOL | SELECT CANDIDATES | TRAIN & DEVELOP FELLOWS | SUPPORT PRINCIPALS |

EVALUATE PROGRAM THROUGHOUT

PRINCIPAL COMPETENCY MODEL

CHAPTER 6
The mission of the RLA programs is to dramatically improve student outcomes and close achievement gaps. They rely on an ongoing data feedback loop to strengthen their own models, and in a departure from other school leader preparation programs, they ultimately hold themselves accountable for the on-the-job performance of their graduates.

Competency Framework

1

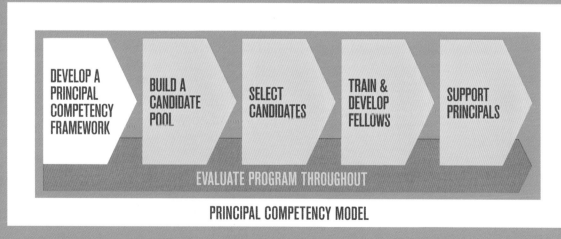

DEVELOP A PRINCIPAL COMPETENCY FRAMEWORK

BUILD A CANDIDATE POOL

SELECT CANDIDATES

TRAIN & DEVELOP FELLOWS

SUPPORT PRINCIPALS

EVALUATE PROGRAM THROUGHOUT

PRINCIPAL COMPETENCY MODEL

1

COMPETENCY FRAMEWORK | RLA programs start by defining a Competency Framework—the set of *skills, knowledge, and dispositions that a principal must have, in his or her context, in order to lead a school effectively to drive high levels of student achievement for all children.* This set of standards uses the school as the lens to identify the most important things high-performing principals must know and be able to do.

The program then takes responsibility for finding and preparing school leaders who can become proficient in these competencies. The Competency Framework creates the guiding goals and provides the structure to coordinate and align all the programmatic elements, systems, and processes. (The Competency Framework outlines the standards for a principal entering a school, not for an aspiring principal candidate entering a program.)

The Competency Framework guides everything from building a candidate pool, to selecting candidates, to training and developing the aspiring leader, to supporting the new principal. Ultimately, the Competency Framework also serves as the key evaluative tool. Thus, the Competency Framework is the foundation and link between all elements of the program. People who are responsible for different components of the program—from selection to coursework to experiential elements of training—align their efforts to the Competency Framework to ensure cohesion.

Each RLA program has created or adopted its own Competency Framework based on its beliefs, its context, and the research base about what is most important for a principal to be effective; though each is unique, there are many similarities.[7]

Looking across several frameworks, you can immediately see that RLA members generally value similar things—*belief and high expectations, resiliency, adult leadership, instructional leadership, self-awareness, openness to learning, and ability to use data to drive instructional improvement*—but also have some variations due to the context of their schools or their theories of action.

After RLA programs define the skills, knowledge, and dispositions of their principals, they carefully work through which of the competencies they believe they can develop within the program time frame using available resources. These areas are reinforced and enhanced with training, development, and support, generally including in-school residency and coursework modules. The competencies that are too time- or resource-intensive to develop (or other qualities a fellow needs as a foundation in order to progress quickly on the learning trajectory) are purposefully included in the programs' selection criteria. Both the Competency Framework and the selection criteria help inform program messages when recruiting candidates.

The Principal Competency Framework

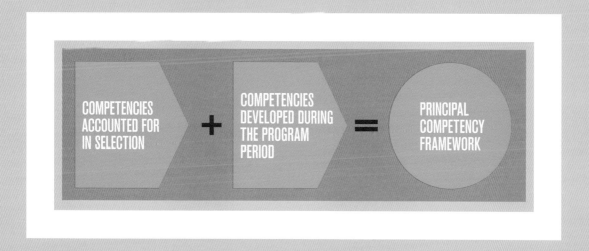

Ultimately, RLA programs recognize that you either need to select for a certain competency or train for that competency if you expect the fellow to have proficiency in the competency by the end of the program.

The Competency Framework is the key evaluative tool for RLA programs for formative and summative evaluations. Most programs create a carefully designed rubric based on the competencies as a tool that allows them to be consistent and explicit as they rate fellows on each component. Initially, after selection, most programs have fellows self-assess against the competencies and then work with a coach and others to incorporate data collected during selection and create a detailed Individualized Learning Plan (ILP) that targets the competencies the fellow needs to develop or enhance. Often this self-assessment happens multiple times a year at certain benchmark points.

During coursework and residency, mapping a fellow's progress against the competencies allows the program to continue to target specific growth areas as well as draw on areas of strength in a fellow's contribution to a residency school site. At the end of the training period, competencies are the standard against which a fellow is measured to determine readiness for a principalship. If the fellow is not proficient in the competencies, he or she may need more time to develop in an assistant principal role, or may not be suited for the principalship. Determining areas in which the fellow is strongest can also help a program guide the person to a principalship in a certain type of school that particularly needs those strengths. Finally, the Competency Framework allows fellows and their programs to pinpoint the areas a fellow will want to grow further as he or she enters the principalship.

New Leaders for New Schools developed the Urban Excellence Framework™ (2008) to guide all of its work, from recruitment and admission to coursework, residency, and support. The Urban Excellence Framework™ (UEF) defines the school-level practices and leadership actions that drive dramatic gains in academic achievement. There are five major categories of school practices and principal actions within the UEF:

▷ Student Achievement-Based Learning and Teaching
▷ Achievement and Belief-Based School-Wide Culture
▷ Personal Leadership
▷ High-Quality Staff Aligned to Vision
▷ Operations and Systems to Help Drive Learning and School Culture

Within each category, there are key levers necessary for any school to make dramatic gains. New Leaders for New Schools focuses on teaching its residents how to "pull" these levers effectively and supports them as principals as they work to do so.

School practices and competencies are defined from a "beginner" level to an "expert" level, assuming it takes many years into the principalship to achieve expert status. Fellows are scored on each of these subcategories using a 10-point scale. This was a shift for New Leaders for New Schools. Previously, its principal Competency Framework rated the top level of 4 as proficient. With the Urban Excellence Framework™, proficiency is now midway through the continuum. Upon admission, New Leaders for New Schools expects fellows to score at least a 3 in each area, and by the time they complete training and become a principal they are expected to score 5 (proficiency). As they develop expertise as a principal, the program anticipates gradual movement from 5 up to 10.

See *Appendix B* for examples of several programs' Competency Frameworks:

The **KIPP School Leadership Program's** *Leadership Framework and Competency Model* describes the competencies and behaviors considered most important to the performance of KIPP principals and other school leaders.

The **NYC Leadership Academy's** Leadership Performance Standards Matrix identifies a set of behaviorally-based performance standards—organized into 12 dimensions—that reflect the attributes of transformational and instructional leaders. The organization uses the Matrix to guide the selection and comprehensive evaluation of participants in its Aspiring Principals Program (APP), and to guide its curricular scope, assignments, and interventions. In order to graduate from the program, APP participants must demonstrate competency in all 12 dimensions.

Program developers themselves can also benefit from Competency Frameworks by using them to measure their own success and be accountable for developing their fellows in each of the specified competency areas. Ultimately, programs would like to get a sense of which competencies are most closely linked with graduates' effectiveness (e.g., positive impact on student achievement, placement as principals, and longevity of effective service) to focus on the highest impact areas in their own selection and training and development.

The **University of Illinois at Chicago** (UIC) recently took more than a year to redesign its program, starting with its Competency Framework. UIC opted to adopt the Chicago Public Schools' Office of Principal Preparation and Development's (CPS OPPD) competencies and success factors as its standard for the first 18 months of the three-year (plus one year for Capstone project/dissertation) Ed.D. program. This document is based on a district analysis of the role of the principal, capturing the strategic activities principals perform and the skills, knowledge, and dispositions required for success.

Using these competencies, UIC worked backward to rethink selection and the training and development components of its program. Each of the UIC courses now has clearly defined competency outcomes that are articulated upfront. All of the courses are aligned to ensure that every competency is accounted for in the sequence. UIC also brought in more practitioners to teach or co-teach classes and worked with existing faculty to integrate more focused, hands-on learning experiences; work with a practitioner; and focus on the competencies. Tremendous cooperation and strong communication systems are necessary to ensure this sort of alignment. At the end of each course, instructors meet together to explicitly sign off on every student's mastery of specific competencies, which are designed to build and progress from course to course.

After fellows have demonstrated proficiency in the CPS OPPD competencies, and most have been placed in a principalship, they move on to a second set of expectations that guide the remainder of the program. UIC is currently finalizing this second set of competencies, using its own standards for UIC's Capstone research dissertation project as well as pieces from the National Board Certification for Principals.

Ultimately it is the quality and thoughtfulness of each RLA program's principal Competency Framework that allows them to craft a well-aligned program, select, train, and develop aspiring principals, and support principals effectively. We refer back to the Competency Frameworks and their central role in guiding RLA program design and delivery throughout this document.

A Look Ahead: Building a Candidate Pool

As RLA programs begin to build a pool of candidates to select from, they draw on their Competency Frameworks to define the skills, knowledge, and dispositions of high-potential recruits.

Building a Candidate Pool

2

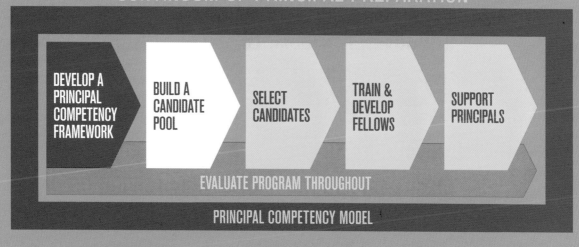

CONTINUUM OF PRINCIPAL PREPARATION

DEVELOP A PRINCIPAL COMPETENCY FRAMEWORK

BUILD A CANDIDATE POOL

SELECT CANDIDATES

TRAIN & DEVELOP FELLOWS

SUPPORT PRINCIPALS

EVALUATE PROGRAM THROUGHOUT

PRINCIPAL COMPETENCY MODEL

2

BUILDING A CANDIDATE POOL | With school districts and charter management organizations across the country grappling with ways to increase the quantity of effective school principals, the RLA aspiring principal programs have made the recruiting of strong candidates a critical step in their overall effort. Traditionally, many principal preparation programs have overlooked recruiting as an important step in the development of principals. RLA programs, on the other hand, rely on *strategic, proactive, and targeted recruiting strategies* to ensure that they have strong candidate pools and pipeline programs from which they can select candidates most likely to thrive in the program and grow into effective principals. Because RLA programs regard school leaders as agents of systematic change within public education, they invest time and resources to identify and attract high-quality candidates, not simply relying on candidates to self-select into programs. Their recruitment techniques are consistently evaluated based on data and adjusted as needed.

Building a Candidate Pool

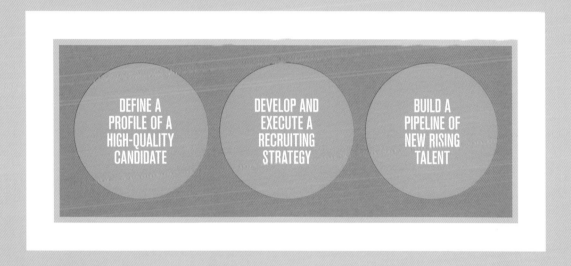

RLA programs have learned—often the hard way—that getting a large number of applicants is not always the best strategy. What is more cost effective and efficient is building the right pool of candidates who are more likely to meet their program's selection criteria and be admitted to the program. Building such a pool requires deliberate action and does not happen merely by passively waiting for candidates to apply or by general marketing efforts.

This chapter outlines how RLA programs generally approach recruiting: including defining upfront their high-quality candidate profile; developing and executing a recruiting strategy that identifies, targets, cultivates, and converts high-potential candidates into applicants; and building a pipeline of new talent going forward. (Selecting candidates from the candidate pool is discussed in the next chapter.)

Learn more in the next chapter.

SEE PAGE 44

G?

In reading this chapter, you may want to reflect back on these Guiding Questions to plan your own recruitment strategy.

> What skills, knowledge, and dispositions (*see the* **Competency Framework** *chapter*) are most desired for your program? Which will candidates need to possess in some depth upon admission and which ones do you plan to develop and reinforce?

> How many quality candidates do you need to apply to yield the number of matriculants you want to enroll in your program? What are your assumptions about the percentage or number of applicants who will meet your selection criteria? What about the percentage or number who, if they receive an offer, will accept?

> Where do you find the quality candidates you want for your program? Which sources yield the highest acceptance rate during selection process?

> How will you define and give identity to your program so candidates understand your approach and can determine if your program is a good fit?

> How will you differentiate high-potential candidates for your program from low-potential candidates and invest recruiting resources accordingly?

> How and when will data be collected and what data will you collect to learn about which strategies are most effective in yielding successful candidates for principals?

Define a Profile of a High-Quality Candidate

As part of recruitment, RLA programs communicate the core competencies and dispositions (based on the Competency Framework) required for a candidate to gain admission to their programs. This profile of an ideal candidate is designed to convey to potential applicants the qualities of an aspiring school leader who has what it takes to improve schools and student outcomes. RLA members want to target and attract the best pool of candidates who are likely to make it through the selection process. By articulating their program's mission, vision, culture, and expectations on the front end as part of recruitment, they strive to help the candidates who are best suited for their program, and likely to succeed in the role of school leader, to self-identify.

How will you translate the skills, knowledge, and dispositions of a successful principal, as mapped out in the Competency Framework, into a high-quality candidate profile?

Which areas do you plan to train and develop and which skills, knowledge, and dispositions must be selected for upfront?

What kind of candidate is the best fit for the program and the likely school placement, taking into account context, culture, and expectations for performance?

K?

In reading this chapter, you may want to reflect back on these Key Questions to plan your own recruitment strategy.

Most importantly, RLA programs seek mission-driven candidates—those people who are committed to dramatic school improvement as demonstrated in improved student outcomes. Candidates need to have that deep commitment and orientation coming into the program. In addition to beliefs and results orientation, two other core competencies stand out in RLA definitions of high-potential recruits: the ability to lead adults; and resilience in the face of obstacles or challenges. For RLA programs these are the qualities that need to be identified during recruitment (and selection), as they are critical to success in RLA programs and schools.

As an example, the **KIPP School Leadership Program** seeks passionate, committed educators to run great public schools in educationally underserved communities. KIPP defines two separate strands in its leadership model: 1) prospective principals being trained to open a new KIPP school; and 2) successor leaders who step into existing KIPP schools. While many of the skills and talents required for these two positions are the same, KIPP makes some distinctions. Founding principals who are expected to start up a new school need to be innovative, flexible, and good communicators. In addition to the key competencies of self-awareness, instructional leadership, and cultural fit, KIPP emphasizes an entrepreneurial approach, resilience, and the ability to deal with ambiguity. Succession principals who inherit built-out staff and full-blown instructional programs have the challenge of hitting the ground running and being skilled in the areas of management and instruction. For these principals, KIPP looks for candidates who demonstrate the ability to manage change, set direction, lead adults and teams, and drive instruction. Messaging these core competencies and the purpose of the program, for KIPP and others, is very important.

As a two-year MBA program, **Rice University's Education Entrepreneurship Program** (REEP) seeks candidates with a very strong instructional foundation because it does not focus on instructional leadership in its training. Instead, it emphasizes leadership development, business training, and education entrepreneurship to help educators become strong, innovative school leaders. REEP is careful to recruit and select teachers who already know what good teaching looks like and who show an ability to diagnose and develop the capacities of others.

RLA programs seek mission-driven candidates—those people who are committed to dramatic school improvement as demonstrated in improved student outcomes.

Develop and Execute a Recruiting Strategy

Typically, RLA programs develop a comprehensive recruiting strategy that includes a variety of tactics to attract high-quality leadership talent to their programs. For many RLA programs, recruitment is an ongoing, year-round process and starts early—often one year or more out before program applications are due. In order to improve their methods from year to year, RLA members collect and regularly review data on their strategies and their success rates.

A good recruiting strategy involves multiple steps, including: 1) projecting need; 2) preparing recruiters (internal and/or external) to promote the program and identify strong potential candidates; 3) establishing an identity; 4) attracting and identifying candidates; 5) determining those with the highest potential; and 6) cultivating and converting high-potential candidates into applicants. Each of these steps is described on the following pages. A complete recruitment strategy sample from **New Leaders for New Schools** that maps out goals, key strategies, and activities to target and leverage talent can be found in *Appendix C*.

Learn more in Appendix C.

SEE PAGE 157

How will you project the number of principals needed year to year? What will be the source(s) of that information?

How will you use that projected number to estimate the ideal size of the candidate pool (which is then significantly narrowed during selection)?

Who within the organization will be responsible for recruitment? How will these people (and any other staff who might interact with potential candidates) be trained to talk confidently about the program model and identify strong candidates?

How will your program get the word out to high-potential candidates? Broad-based strategies? Targeted strategies? Or some combination?

How will your program determine which talent sources are most effective?

How will data be compiled in order to determine high-potential candidates?

How will you cultivate individual relationships in order to convert strong candidates into actual applicants?

How will you think of "return on investment" on recruitment expenses? What is the best way for your program to measure recruiting costs: cost per applicant, per matriculant, other?

In reading this chapter, you may want to reflect back on these Key Questions to plan your own recruitment strategy.

Projecting Need

As a first step, RLA programs take a sophisticated, data-based approach to projecting the numbers of principals needed to serve their networks. Their goal is to try to prepare enough (or a targeted percentage of) principals to help meet their needs, or their district and charter school partners' needs. That means not only anticipating the number of principals to be hired at least two—and up to five—years out but the types of school placement opportunities: elementary, secondary, start-up, turnaround, etc. As much as possible, these projections should account for principal retirements, student population shifts, turnover/replacement needs, the initiation of special programs or schools (e.g. creation of small high schools from large schools), and other changes.

Once those numbers have been projected to the best of a program's ability, the program providers can anticipate the desired number of graduates and plan backward to determine the number of candidates they need to select and train. Knowing not all of the candidates recruited will be selected, programs try to estimate the number of candidates they need to recruit to ultimately yield the number they aspire to train and graduate. While RLA programs want to recruit only the highest-caliber candidates, they balance this with the objective of training enough principals to meet demand. As a result, during both recruitment and selection, RLA members try not to exclude those who they believe, with the right training and support, will become very effective school leaders.

Figure 2 on page 29 illustrates a hypothetical, but not atypical, relationship between the recruitment and selection processes. Programs build their candidate pools over time during the recruitment period with the intention of securing a certain number of actual applicants. They know that that applicant pool will be narrowed significantly during the selection process as lower-potential candidates are winnowed out, resulting in a small number of actual matriculants.

RLA programs endeavor during recruitment to be transparent about what it takes to be a strong and effective principal in order to identify and attract individuals who possess the right skills, dispositions, and talents to their programs. They try to find the right balance of recruiting a diverse representation of applicants, while also focusing on those with the greatest potential for success. In fact, while low selectivity rates may seem desirable (indicating competitiveness), as RLA programs have become more established and successful in recruiting strong pools of candidates, their selectivity rates have gone up—moving from admitting 6-10 percent of applicants to 20 percent, for example. This is an indication that a program is successfully recruiting the right people from the start.

> RLA programs want to invest their resources in the strongest prospects in order to convert them into actual applicants.

Relationship Between Recruitment and Selection

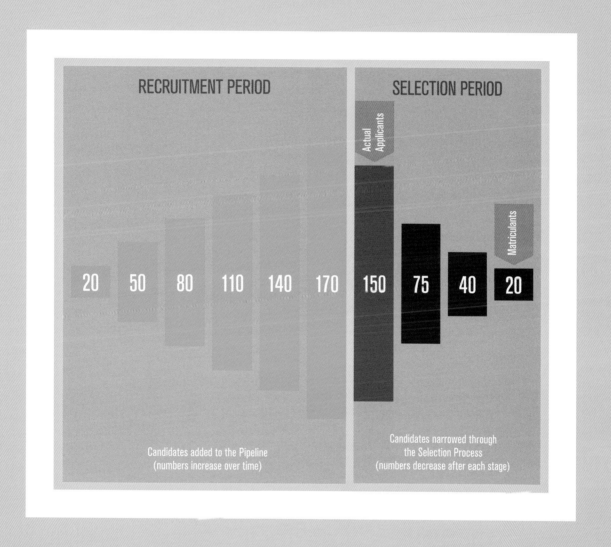

Preparing Recruiters

All of the RLA programs dedicate staff time to recruiting, and some have full-time recruiters in place. RLA programs employ high-quality, trained recruitment personnel who can articulate program expectations and masterfully vet for targeted competencies, using the high-potential candidate profile and the selection criteria.

To do this effectively, staff, as well as program alumni or others doing recruitment, need to have a deep understanding of the program model. To ensure that there is consistent messaging and coordination, RLA programs invest time and resources in training people how to frame the program, use marketing and informational materials and other resources, and respond to commonly asked questions.

As RLA programs scale up, they often find themselves overwhelmed with a constant flood of information requests, phone calls, and emails. In response, many programs have produced written and easily accessible documentation about their programs, available on detailed home web pages, such as program overviews and Frequently Asked Questions. To ensure a coordinated and timely response, programs sometimes establish a dedicated email address for information requests.

Establishing an Identity

RLA programs clearly articulate and communicate the distinct qualities of their program models in order to attract high-quality candidates. They do not advertise themselves as generic principal preparation programs, but instead highlight their individual missions, goals, and strengths.

The advantage of establishing a clear identity is that it helps attract candidates with the right fit to the program, thereby limiting the resources spent on weeding out the wrong candidates. For new programs that do not yet have an established identity or that are expanding into new communities, endorsements from highly regarded education networks or school reform agencies with a similar vision of improving student achievement outcomes can be extremely helpful in getting the word out and drawing high-quality applicants.

During its information sessions, the **NYC Leadership Academy** asks potential candidates to consider seriously whether its Aspiring Principals Program (APP) will be the right fit for them. These sessions, which are led by program staff and include alumni, offer prospective candidates an authentic representation of APP. In addition to a comprehensive overview of the program, there is frank and candid discussion regarding program demands and expectations. The goal is to identify candidates passionately committed to the hard work of improving student outcomes in high-need schools and to discourage those merely looking for a job or a next step in their careers. Therefore, staff members ensure that prospective participants walk away with a strong sense of the program's rigor, high expectations and explicit social justice agenda, which requires candidates to accept principalships where their services are most needed. Similarly, program alumni share the challenges they faced both during the program and, on the ground, as new principals. Equipped with this information, prospective candidates can determine whether or not the program is the right path for them.

> RLA programs rely on strategic, proactive, and targeted recruiting strategies to ensure that they have strong candidate pools and pipeline programs from which they can select candidates most likely to thrive in the program and grow into effective principals.

Attracting and Identifying Candidates: Broad-Based Strategies

RLA programs use broad-based marketing strategies to get the word out about organization mission, features and goals of the program, and their track record of success. While word of mouth is often a good resource for RLA members, most use at least some *broad-based* strategies that cast a wide net to publicize their programs.

Traditional strategies have included posting flyers, bulk mailings, print ads, email blasts, job postings, and organizational websites. In general, RLA programs have not found hosting open job fairs or manning booths at national conferences to yield very many high-potential candidates. These days, RLA programs agree that the most cost effective and efficient broad-based methods include well-organized, information-heavy websites; e-banner ad placements; mass emails; search engine optimization strategies; and electronic networking and social media channels (Facebook, Twitter). This new emphasis on electronic media helps RLA programs target certain groups and demographics more easily and is often less expensive and more effective than print ads or other high-cost, hard copy alternatives.

Attracting and Identifying Candidates: Targeted Strategies

Most RLA programs go beyond broad-based to *targeted* strategies that focus on specific high-quality sources of candidates or individual candidates they learn about. Targeted strategies are used to identify strong candidates and to take the time to court them to apply. While these high-touch activities are more resource intensive, many RLA programs find they pay off and yield the bulk of the candidates who are ultimately selected for their programs.

Targeted strategies include:
- Soliciting nominations from successful principals, trainers, coaches, district staff in schools, and professional development staff in target districts/CMOs or region
- Identifying high-performing teachers or assistant principals (e.g. award winners, high-impact on student achievement) and contacting them
- Soliciting recommendations from program alumni, current coaches/mentors
- Soliciting recommendations from local organizations (teacher groups, community-based partners, business organizations, professional associations, etc.)

RLA programs nurture these personal relationships with practitioners in the field as they tend to generate highly qualified prospects, and the nominators serve as excellent spokespeople for the program. This network works on behalf of the program, encouraging talented teachers, teacher leaders (e.g. department chairs, team leaders, grade-level chairs), and assistant principals to apply, which saves recruitment costs. RLA programs are careful to build relationships with these individuals and cultivate them as talent spotters. They reach out to them on a regular basis to solicit candidate names. In turn, the programs keep them engaged in the program and up-to-date on their recruitment prospects. These external partners—nominators, referral groups, and talent scouts—may be invited to RLA training events and/or included in the selection process to help them gain an in-depth understanding of the program model and the profile of the desired candidate.

In light of this lesson about the impact of personal relationships, some RLA programs have started community campaigns to leverage relationships and connections. For instance, the **New Leaders for New Schools'** Milwaukee Power of One campaign sends the message that one person can make a difference by nominating recruits who have the capacity and the drive to change a school. The program asks for single nominations of candidates who fit the program profile. New Leaders for New Schools reminds nominators that their single nomination has the power to change the lives of hundreds or thousands of students and their families.

When the **NYC Leadership Academy** was launched in 2003, the significant amount of publicity generated helped the organization attract many high-quality candidates without targeted recruitment work. Over time, however, the NYC Leadership Academy has adopted a targeted approach for recruiting a diverse pool of high-potential candidates. In addition to broad-based recruitment strategies, the organization relies on a network of nominators—some 500 strong—that it has cultivated and calls on to nominate high-potential candidates for its Aspiring Principals Program (APP). This network includes APP graduates (representing some 200 principals), other principals, superintendents, district leaders across the New York City public school system, and NYC Leadership Academy staff. Network members are essentially talent scouts and APP ambassadors. What makes the network effective is that its members know the APP program model well and thus, are adept at identifying candidates who are well-matched to the program's mission, vision, and rigor. Network members are also actively engaged in the recruitment process: They host information sessions and follow up with candidates to engage and nurture their interest in the program. Because many network members have direct relationships with the prospective candidates, they are extremely effective recruiters who are able to help candidates determine whether the program is right for them. Without the network, the NYC Leadership Academy would expend significantly greater resources to identify quality candidates and encourage them to apply. The NYC Leadership Academy attributes its success in recruiting people of color to individuals within its network of nominators who are committed to mentoring high-potential candidates of color.

Sources of Candidates

RLA programs rely on many sources to find high-quality candidates:

Within the district or CMO: RLA programs target individuals already in the district(s) or charter network in which they prepare principals. The benefit of drawing from a local, internal pool is that programs have immediate access to candidates' work history and supervisors. Additionally, candidates have the benefit of knowing the district culture and operating procedures, which may smooth their transition into the principalship. However, if the district/CMO is seeking to implement substantial changes in procedures and culture, internal candidates, accustomed to previous expectations, may have a more difficult time making adjustments. Programs need to take district context into consideration when considering this source.

Outside the immediate district or CMO: Some individuals may be willing to relocate. Some RLA programs target staff from Title 1 schools who demonstrate success with high-need students. RLA programs analyze the sources of successful matriculants who come from locations outside their immediate territory and may recruit from these new feeder markets. Broad-based marketing efforts help attract candidates outside the local area, as do partnerships with regional and national organizations that can help spread the word.

Teacher and teacher leader networks: RLA programs tap high-quality networks of talented teachers and teacher leaders. In particular, RLA members often focus on organizations that exhibit a similar mission-driven focus, such as Teach For America, The New Teacher Project, and the Peace Corps. Teach For America is a natural source for many RLA programs, for example, as it emphasizes leadership skills upon entry, and currently more than 500 corps members are sitting principals across the country. RLA members also partner with other high-quality professional development organizations and nonprofits that have access to pools of high-quality teachers and teacher leaders.

Professionals who are not presently in education: RLA programs are also cognizant of tapping candidates who have previously taught, but have temporarily left the field of education and gained leadership or organizational management skills in other arenas and/or obtained professional degrees in leadership and management. This group can be harder to reach, which is why programs use wide-net strategies to put the word out to MBA alumni and the corporate ranks.

Underrepresented groups: To recruit more candidates of color, RLA members often reach out to local identity- or community-based organizations both within education and the business sector. Examples of professional organizations include the Hispanic Educators Association, the National Association for Bilingual Education, and the National Alliance of Black School Educators. RLA members do their best to differentiate their marketing to target underrepresented groups, including follow-up to make sure candidates are aware of the program and the application deadlines. One RLA member recently started a communication campaign with Historically Black Colleges and Universities in hopes of recruiting more African American males, and some programs have created partnerships with African American fraternities and sororities to spread the word about their programs and identify candidates.

Determining Candidates with Highest Potential for Selection

Once candidates are identified, RLA programs spend time getting to know them through a review of background information, informal conversations, and contact with their supervisors (where appropriate) and others who have knowledge of their work history and performance.

This early evidence-gathering helps programs tease out as much information as possible to determine which candidates are high-potential. RLA programs want to invest their resources in the strongest prospects in order to convert them into actual applicants, as cultivation and conversion often require a real investment.

Before applications are submitted, **New Leaders for New Schools** gathers evidence to determine which candidates are high-potential. This might begin with a résumé review or conversations to search for key indicators, which New Leaders for New Schools data have shown to be correlated with past candidate and matriculant success (these indicators include: past experience leading adults, discussion of results with students, and/or connections to a mission-aligned organization such as Teach For America, The New Teacher Project, Peace Corps, or AmeriCorps). Those who have strong backgrounds aligned with the New Leaders for New Schools profile receive follow-up calls to build their interest and to probe for core competencies such as candidate beliefs, results orientation, adult leadership experience, teaching and learning, and resilience.

New Leaders for New Schools also makes good use of general information sessions, using round-robins and other formats to get the participants talking about their *beliefs* (Why do you want to be an urban school principal?), *results orientation* (What is your biggest accomplishment?), and *teaching and learning capacity* (How do you utilize data around goal setting?). This information is added to the candidate's profile in the database and used to organize the candidates into four tiers. New Leaders for New Schools can then better manage who they pursue and encourage to apply, allocating resources accordingly. The top potential candidates (tiers 1 and 2) receive more high-touch services and attention, such as professional development events (webinars and in-person) to expose them to the program, school visits, and match-ups with New Leaders for New Schools alumni.

Candidate tiering is not a system to weed out candidates. Any candidate may submit an application. This structure is designed to maximize recruiter time and focus, as well as organizational efforts and dollars. The candidate management system is new and the program is grappling with how, and if, the tiered ratings should be included as part of the candidate's profile during the selection process. Currently this information is segregated from selection so as not to bias that process.

For many RLA programs, recruitment is an ongoing, year-round process and starts early—often one year or more out before program applications are due.

Cultivating and Converting High-Potential Candidates

As part of the cultivating process, RLA programs do their best to respond to any individual concerns or hesitations that high-potential candidates might express. For instance, if candidates have families and are concerned about the length of the intensive summer training, a program might have them talk with alumni who had similar situations and can make them feel more comfortable about the time commitment. Program staff may invite top candidates to visit a school to see an effective principal in action and get excited by the opportunity to make a difference for underserved students. They may be invited to attend a professional development course to get a better sense of the program and its fellows. Staff members may also connect candidates with alumni who can talk about their own experiences in the program. Program staff or candidate nominators typically contact candidates on a regular basis throughout the recruiting process to answer any questions and encourage them to apply, often working with them right up to the deadline for applications. Candidates may receive newsletters, information bulletins, and other program materials. All of these activities and outreach efforts are designed to make sure the candidate has all of the relevant information needed to make a decision about whether to apply.

RLA programs are very aware that these are two-way conversations and interviews. The program is trying to entice the candidate to apply or self-select out. The candidate is taking stock of the program and weighing the benefits. Strong candidates will likely have a lot of education and work options available to them, and therefore programs need to be ready to court them to some degree. Programs use their databases to track these interactions and schedule next steps to ensure the candidate experience is positive and appropriately timed.

RLA programs have also learned that some of the strongest-fitting candidates do not always see themselves as future principals, sometimes because of their experience and sometimes because of their own limited perception of the principalship, especially if they have not seen effective principals in action. RLA programs try to help these candidates better understand how their skills fit the modern principalship. Sometimes, programs engage alumni to talk with these candidates or facilitate visits to schools where a program graduate is principal to help the candidate understand the opportunity and learn more about the network. They may need to be approached multiple times before they see how their skills would be a good fit for school leadership in today's context. While ultimately, candidates must want to do the job of the principal and decide this for themselves, RLA programs are willing to invest the resources to help candidates explore the role and understand their fit if they believe the individuals are a strong match for the program.

Build a Pipeline
of New Rising Talent

RLA programs have an interest in increasing the size of the candidate pool while also strengthening its quality. Many have come to recognize the importance of building a pipeline of talent to feed into their programs. Eager, aspiring leaders are identified early and given leadership development opportunities to build their skill sets *before* they apply to programs. Also, pipeline development helps RLA programs increase their diversity since underrepresented groups can be specifically targeted for development.

In reading this chapter, you may want to reflect back on these Key Questions to plan your own recruitment strategy.

If recruits do not fit your desired profile, how can you work with district/CMO partners to establish a leadership pipeline to develop talent? Are there ways in your Competency Framework and/or training to address patterns of gaps in skills and knowledge that prevented candidates from being admitted to the program?

How can you begin to identify and develop teacher leaders on campuses in your district/CMO partners that possess leadership potential and aspirations?

What kind of feedback do you give candidates who show promise but need additional development and experience to be ready?

Will your program offer skill building and other resources to those candidates that you would like to see re-apply? How will you tailor those services and maintain contact until the following admissions cycle?

The **KIPP School Leadership Program** has been training prospective principals for its network of schools since 2000. As the network has grown, KIPP has recognized the value of reaching deeper down into the schools and giving teachers and other school leaders the skills needed to share in leadership and sustain the pipeline of future principals over time. Through its School Leadership Pathways Program, KIPP offers three additional pathways that develop leaders at multiple levels within KIPP schools. The purpose is to develop shared leadership within KIPP schools and to grow a pipeline of leaders who can be tapped for increasing leadership opportunities, including the principalship. Each pathway is based on the KIPP School Leadership Competency Model that outlines the competencies and behaviors considered most important to develop at that stage of the leadership pipeline. For each of the programs, applicants must receive a formal nomination from their current school leader and/or regional leader.

Teacher Leaders: Aimed at teachers who serve in roles such as grade-level chair or department chair, this program is designed to help teachers gain a school-level perspective on improving instruction. It emphasizes two big themes: 1) team leadership and management of adults; and 2) instructional leadership. During the year-long program, the cohort meets three times for long weekend trainings.

Leadership Team: Aimed at emerging senior leaders in the school (i.e., staff currently holding assistant principal, dean of instruction, or dean of culture positions), this pathway focuses on developing: 1) critical thinking, problem solving, and decision making; 2) communication, impact, and influence; 3) performance management; and 4) instructional leadership. School leaders select the participants, who delve into a year-long experience that includes a three-day orientation in May, a summer institute, and three long weekend trainings. During the summer, participants attend five weeks of intensive leadership development.

Succession Principal Preparation: Aimed at leaders who plan to assume the role of school leader at an existing school within the next 18 months, this pathway focuses on: 1) direction-setting; 2) operational management; 3) change management; and 4) stakeholder management. Like the Leadership Team model, it is a year-long experience including an orientation in May and five weeks of intensive leadership development in the summer.

These pathway programs create a natural pipeline of emerging leaders within the school network who understand the unique KIPP culture and can lead KIPP schools. Two out of three KIPP new founding and sustaining principals are internal KIPP community candidates. KIPP schools also benefit by having a deeper bench of people who possess the skills and tools needed to lead teams effectively—with a common language about instructional leadership and performance management.

RLA programs work with their district and CMO partners to create and increase opportunities for teachers and others to take on significant leadership roles earlier in their careers. By proactively increasing the opportunities teachers have to lead other adults, districts and schools can tap the creativity and passion of educators at all levels and set the expectation that all staff members are instructional leaders. RLA programs also often take the opportunity to work with talented candidates of color who show promising leadership skills to ensure that they have a diverse candidate pool to recruit from. Obviously, some people will fall out of the pipeline as it progresses, but providing chances for individuals to test their leadership mettle will help identify future leaders and nurture their skills. RLA programs cultivate relationships with districts and CMOs to encourage internal talent development that not only strengthens the schools and helps current students but also creates a natural pipeline for aspiring principal programs.

Pipeline development efforts vary based on program context. For district-based programs, such as *Gwinnett County Public Schools*, pipeline development is a logical step to cultivating human capital. For national programs that do not draw from a particular district or network of schools, some creativity and an investment of resources is needed to cultivate an ongoing talent supply. (Both models are described in the examples below.)

EXAMPLE

Gwinnett County Public Schools, located outside Atlanta, is developing its own pipeline of home-grown talent to lead its more than 120 schools. In January 2010, the district created the Quality-Plus Leader Academy Aspiring Leader Program (ALP) to identify teachers who aspire to entry-level school leadership (either as an assistant principal (AP) or an administrative intern). The ALP is designed to increase the quality of the applicant pool for the Aspiring Principal Program (APP).

The program focuses on areas such as: leadership; curriculum, instruction, and assessment; human capital management; and operations management. The first cohort participated in six all-day sessions taught by in-district instructors. ALP employs engaging and real-life teaching strategies including case studies, simulations, debates, and role-playing activities to immerse teachers in the challenges and demands of the AP position. Principals are already seeing an impact in the schools; program participants are taking on leadership roles and making a difference for students.

After completing the coursework, participants are expected to complete a three-week residency during summer school, working with a facilitator/coach to hone their skills. This hands-on experience gives teachers the opportunity to assess student progress and achievement; interact with teaching staff, parents, and students; and gain experience in operational management. Program completers are eligible to apply for assistant principal placement within Gwinnett County Public Schools.

Gwinnett has long had a culture of continuous improvement. District leadership expects principals to develop and build leadership in the talent around them for the benefit of teaching and learning. This expectation is constantly stated publicly, modeled by the superintendent, and principals are held accountable in their evaluations. Interest and enthusiasm for the ALP program is evident: in just the first year, 250 teachers applied, 36 were selected to participate, and 18 have been appointed to assistant principal jobs.

EXAMPLE

For RLA programs such as **New Leaders for New Schools** that do not draw from an institutionalized network or district of schools, the issue is maintaining a steady supply of high-quality candidates. Rather than letting strong prospects, that made it to the final stages of selection but are not quite ready, walk away, some of the New Leaders for New Schools regions are engaging and supporting them to build a future pipeline.

Right after the conclusion of admissions, candidates who were not selected but are deemed to be possibly one to three years away from being "ready" are given one-on-one feedback about strengths and areas that need development. New Leaders for New Schools counsels them on next steps and helps them to map out individual development plans. For those currently working in schools that may have poor principals where they may not be able to strengthen their skills, candidates might be coached to find new professional opportunities where they can grow. Others might be counseled to stay in their job but gain leadership experience. In some cases, the program might engage the candidate's principal to explore growth opportunities within the school for the candidate.

RLA members are purposeful in capturing and using data generated during the recruitment process to become more strategic in identifying and attracting top-notch applicants.

Some New Leaders for New Schools regions have created formal programs to give candidates access to resources (newsletters, books, reading lists) and further training and development opportunities (workshops, book study groups, diagnostic team school visits, classroom observations) to strengthen their skills. The opportunities afforded candidates are closely mapped to their needs identified through the selection process. A candidate needing further development in his/her instructional leadership might be offered a classroom observation, workshops on teaching, and an opportunity to see other high-performing classrooms. Someone needing more adult leadership might be assisted with securing more opportunities in their job and offered workshops that focus on communication skills, team building, and relationship development.

While many of these pipeline development programs appear to be a costly approach, some RLA programs see it as a reallocation of resources—moving away from a more costly broad-sweep recruiting effort of national conferences and print ads to a more targeted strategy of grooming high-potential candidates and keeping them in the pipeline. This is in line with district efforts to develop more integrated human capital strategies to ensure a constant supply of talented teachers and school leaders.

COST AND RESOURCE ALLOCATION CONSIDERATIONS

Programs need to be cognizant of the resources and staff time required to implement a recruitment strategy. Costs vary depending on the method employed. There are onetime development costs to design an appealing and informative website, with ongoing maintenance and updates required. Creating a solid candidate management system/database can also require an investment of resources, especially if the system is particularly sophisticated, customized, or has broader functionality. Dedicating staff to recruiting requires salary allocation for recruiting and is usually the most cost-intensive ongoing cost.

Recruiting strategies vary in cost.
▷ Email blasts are not expensive but require staff time to generate up-to-date contact lists.
▷ Newspaper advertisements can be very costly.
▷ Facebook and Twitter are low-cost options.
▷ Information sessions can be very inexpensive if you have donated space, but if you have to rent space to host them and decide to provide food, the costs add up quickly.

Whatever strategies are deployed need to be monitored to determine if the costs involved justify the yield. High-cost, low-yield methods should be abandoned in favor of higher-yield approaches.

RLA programs have chosen to implement differentiated recruitment strategies that require an investment of resources. This high-touch, personalized approach requires a significant amount of staff time to identify and cultivate top candidates. While not abandoning broad-based marketing, many programs have reallocated resources to invest more heavily in a more-targeted strategy of grooming high-potential candidates, which they believe pays off in the caliber of candidates coming into their programs.

Evaluation and Assessment of Recruitment Practices

RLA members are purposeful in capturing and using data generated during the recruitment process to become more strategic in identifying and attracting top-notch applicants. This information is fed into databases—some of which are very sophisticated and customized, others simpler—to build a profile of every prospective recruit that includes résumés, a record of conversations, impressions gained during information sessions, etc. By collecting this information, programs can manage the recruitment process and expend resources on those candidates who demonstrate the most promise. Programs that are able to compile profiles of candidates early in the process can differentiate their recruiting strategies to focus on those who are high-potential.

The comprehensive candidate management system also allows programs to determine which talent sources yield the best candidates—to improve efficiencies and outcomes of the outreach and cultivation process from year to year. RLA members have learned that taking the time upfront to create a robust data system pays off in identifying prospective talent and honing the recruitment process over time.

In reading this chapter, you may want to reflect back on these Key Questions to plan your own recruitment strategy.

What metrics are needed to measure the success of particular recruitment strategies and sources? Number of prospects, number of applicants generated, number of conversions, etc.?

How will you capture information on candidates' skills, knowledge, and dispositions as they relate to the selection criteria during recruitment?

How will you track your actions and processes to know which ones are most effective for identifying and attracting candidates? Targeted marketing efforts? Word of mouth? Strong talent sources?

What strategies are most effective in getting strong applicants to apply? How much time and resources are required to do this cultivation and conversion work?

What are the implications for future recruitment efforts?

Lessons Learned

The RLA members have come to recognize the importance of recruitment and the development of clear pipelines to attract the right number of top-quality candidates. We encourage program providers to evaluate their own circumstances of supply and demand and to identify high-yield sources of talent that will provide the right number of high-quality candidates. Building a data system to effectively measure outputs and results takes time, but is necessary to generate the right information and pays great dividends. Programs may want to consider these key lessons:

1. It is important to *attract candidates who fit your program model*. This requires establishing an identity for the program in order to help candidates match themselves appropriately. Invest in identifying and individually recruiting high-potential candidates; don't expect enough high-potential ones to come to your program on their own.

2. *Start building adequate data systems* that generate information on the success of individual recruitment strategies. Gathering details on various talent sources, candidate profiles, training needs, placement data, and impact on the schools will help improve your process. Recruitment strategies may need to undergo reevaluation and adjustment on a regular basis. What worked one, three, or five years ago may not work in the current environment.

3. *Don't jump into recruitment without understanding the local supply/demand equation* and designing a talent recruitment and long-term pipeline strategy that makes sense for your context and aligns to your organizational goals.

4. *Focus on sources that yield talented candidates*; don't squander time and resources on low-yield sources. For example, one RLA member learned that parochial and private school principals have a vested interest in keeping and growing their own talent and that staff from these schools often lack experience closing student achievement gaps in urban school environments. For these reasons, targeting private and parochial schools did not yield good-fit candidates.

5. *Mobilize program alumni as ambassadors and talent scouts.* They know the program model and what it takes to succeed on the job.

6. *Use the data and information gathered during the recruitment and selection phases to build pipelines*, taking advantage of the time and resources already invested in high-potential candidates.

7. *Recruitment strategies may need to be targeted in order to generate a diverse mix of candidates.* Programs need to be proactive in building candidate pools that have a wide representation of demographics (race and gender), school level (elementary and secondary), professional experience, etc.

A Look Ahead: Selecting Candidates

Recruitment melds into the topic of our next chapter, Selecting Candidates. Once the pool of candidates is in place, RLA programs use a team of selectors and a rigorous process to determine which candidates are best aligned to the program mission, have the skills, knowledge, and dispositions to succeed, and can manage the steep learning curve to prepare for the principalship.

Selecting Candidates

3

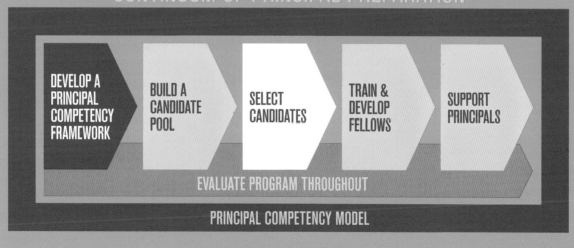

CONTINUUM OF PRINCIPAL PREPARATION

| DEVELOP A PRINCIPAL COMPETENCY FRAMEWORK | BUILD A CANDIDATE POOL | SELECT CANDIDATES | TRAIN & DEVELOP FELLOWS | SUPPORT PRINCIPALS |

EVALUATE PROGRAM THROUGHOUT

PRINCIPAL COMPETENCY MODEL

3

SELECTING CANDIDATES | RLA programs are highly selective and establish clear criteria and rigorous processes to evaluate applicants. For these programs, a review of past experiences and educational credentials is insufficient to determine which applicants have what it takes to develop quickly in the program and succeed in the challenging role of school principal. The RLA programs use a multi-step process that includes experiential events in which candidates are expected to demonstrate their skills, knowledge, and dispositions, aligned with the Competency Framework. It is through these carefully sequenced interactions that the programs can determine which applicants demonstrate the orientations, values, and beliefs that are so important to the principalship. The process is designed to be as objective as possible, relying on trained selectors who use common tools and instruments to evaluate applicants.

The Selection Process

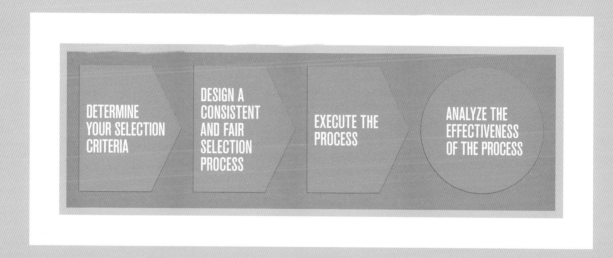

The recruiting and pipeline development process creates a pool of candidates. Selection narrows the pool by using a variety of activities and events to assess how well each individual applicant fits the selection criteria and demonstrates readiness for a set of developmental experiences, which in turn will prepare the candidate for the principalship. A data-driven approach to admitting candidates gives programs the best assurance that their fellows will succeed in the program, become effective principals, and achieve their ultimate objective: exceptional student achievement gains.

SEE PAGE 16

Learn more in the Competency Framework chapter.

RLA programs use different strategies to assess candidates on their skills, knowledge, and dispositions as defined in the Competency Framework (see the *Competency Framework* chapter). While RLA programs reinforce all the skills and dispositions of effective principals during their training, they recognize that these skills, knowledge, and dispositions need to be present to varying degrees at the time of selection; some require full or close to full proficiency before the program begins, while others can be developed during the program.

The RLA programs' commitment to finding talented and passionate people who can ensure that all children are learning in their schools drives every element of their selection process. They depart from traditional admissions processes that rely primarily on paper-based information documenting previous educational experience and accomplishments. Instead, these programs construct carefully sequenced and rigorous selection experiences that require candidates *to demonstrate their skills and dispositions through real-time performance-based assessments* aligned with the required selection criteria. By testing candidates' responses through multiple activities, programs gain a deep understanding of their candidates' capacities and the alignment of their stated beliefs with their actions. Each activity addresses one or more selection criteria so that programs get a complete picture of a candidate and can accurately determine readiness and fit for the program.

SEE PAGE 20

Learn more in the Building a Candidate Pool chapter.

Although RLA programs go to extraordinary lengths to find the right number of candidates to match the projected need, they are willing to admit fewer participants rather than lower their selection standard. As discussed in the *Building a Candidate Pool* chapter, RLA programs emphasize the quality of applicants more than the total number. The stakes of ensuring children a high-quality education are simply too high to enroll participants who do not show evidence that they will ultimately succeed in the principalship at the end of the training program. (However, districts/CMOs still need to fill their positions and, therefore, they may have to recruit high-quality candidates from other sources.)

The remainder of this chapter outlines some clear steps that RLA programs undertake as part of selection, starting with determining selection criteria and designing a selection process, and then moving to the execution of that process and an analysis of its effectiveness.

RLA programs are highly selective and establish clear criteria and rigorous processes to evaluate applicants.

Considering your context, what do you want your graduates to achieve? How will you plan backward from this goal to devise selection criteria and how will the selection criteria be aligned to your Competency Framework?

Have you distinguished between what competencies are desired upfront before the aspiring principals enter your program and those that can be honed through training and development?

How will you use each stage of the selection process to gather evidence to determine which candidates are the best fit for your program?

What tools, procedures, and selector training are needed to ensure that candidates are rated consistently and fairly throughout the various stages of the selection process? How will scoring be normed?

In order to move through the selection process stages, will candidates need to have minimum scores on specific criteria or only a high overall score? Will final decisions be made based on a compilation of scores across phases or an overall score in the final stage (or some hybrid)? Will certain selection criteria have minimum score requirements in the final stage?

Do you have the systems in place to capture relevant data throughout all stages of the selection process that will generate valuable information about your applicant pool?

What resources (e.g., funds, time, staff capacity) do you have to dedicate to selection? How much of your overall program investment will be used on selection versus other program elements? What is the cost versus benefit analysis of this investment?

G?

In reading this chapter, you may want to reflect back on these Guiding Questions to plan your own selection process.

Determine Your Selection Criteria

RLA members derive their selection criteria from the Competency Framework. The Competency Framework outlines the skills, knowledge, and dispositions necessary for a leader to achieve dramatic academic gains with students (see the *Competency Framework* chapter). Selection is the point of entry into the training program—not into the principalship. Therefore, the selection criteria are a subset of the requirements outlined in the Competency Framework—the starting point when an individual enters the principal preparation program.

SEE PAGE 16

Learn more in the Competency Framework chapter.

In addition to prioritizing competencies that align with the actions of high-performing principals, RLA programs take into account the context in which they operate. Some programs work at a national scale; others are district- or university-based. Some concentrate on turnaround school placements, others serve charter networks. Alignment of selection criteria for program purpose and program context is important.

RLA programs invest a lot of time and energy in designing clear selection criteria that lay out the critical skills and dispositions that a candidate should have at the outset, prior to the program's investment of training, in order to become an effective leader. RLA programs not only seek candidates who have the right foundation of incoming skills, knowledge, and, dispositions, but who demonstrate the capacity to learn quickly to become proficient within the program time frame. As discussed in the *Building a Candidate Pool* chapter, some of these qualities must be solidly intact upon entering the program (because they are difficult or highly resource-intensive to develop), others the programs are willing and able to reinforce and enhance significantly with training, development, and support. Most RLA programs aim to yield at the end of the selection process a cohort with a solid foundation of skills and dispositions that can be developed within just one year for the principalship. A few programs have longer training programs.

SEE PAGE 20

Learn more in the Building a Candidate Pool chapter.

As mission-driven organizations committed to driving dramatic change in schools, RLA members unanimously point to "belief," "urgency," "results orientation" and "resiliency" as being non-negotiable in candidates, with "belief" being the most important quality.

Belief and personal responsibility for every child to achieve at a high level, even if they enter the school significantly below grade level. Has a "whatever it takes" attitude and holds self accountable for dramatically improving individual student outcomes. This philosophy/attitude drives the work of effective principals and establishes the expectation for all the adults in the building.

Urgency, insistent focus on getting results quickly. Does not tolerate wasting time or focusing on adult issues over students' needs, and aligns all efforts to expedite student learning and success.

Results orientation for achieving goals and outcomes for students. Takes personal responsibility for achieving outcomes for students. Maintains focus on results, not just the process and inputs.

Resiliency to recover from setbacks and keep moving forward. Ability to adapt to adversity and ambiguity, try new approaches, and keep at it. Remains relentless in the pursuit of the goals for students in the face of challenges and setbacks.

Because these characteristics reflect deeply embedded orientations that are complex and take time to change and develop, RLA programs put the most weight during selection on these intrinsic qualities and orientations. Throughout the selection process, RLA organizations are extremely wary of candidates who indicate signs of misalignment with their core beliefs.

In addition to the dispositions above, all RLA programs agree that candidates must demonstrate some adult leadership skills to be selected into their programs. While RLA programs require different levels of strength in the *adult leadership* skills for program entry, all underscore that leaders' beliefs, urgency, results orientation, and resilience must be coupled with adult leadership skills. An effective principal is one who can translate belief into practice through other adults. Without adult leadership skills, belief and urgency can merely result in a hard-working, driven principal who lacks the ability to organize other adults to improve student learning. Since a principal cannot do the work alone, a determined leader can fail if he or she does not know how to leverage the other adults to get the work done. In many schools, the principal has to change existing staff members' attitudes, beliefs, skills, and priorities—requiring strong adult leadership, communication, and interpersonal skills. As passionate as a leader might be and as much as he or she might love working with children, RLA programs find that that is not enough—their principal candidates must want to organize and lead adults for the benefit of children, and their strongest principals do this exceptionally well.

While RLA programs agree on the priorities cited above, they vary in their training strengths, as well as in the resources available to devote to these capacities. Programs are careful to select candidates who already have certain qualities and skills if they do not intend to focus on them through training.

Almost all of the RLA programs put a high premium on *teaching and learning*, recognizing the importance of the principalship in assessing learning, providing feedback, using data, and establishing a culture of rigor and high expectations. In fact, **New Leaders for New Schools** found in a review of its selection processes that too many applicants were making it to the final stages of selection only to then be denied because they did not meet the non-negotiable score for teaching and learning. As a result, New Leaders for New Schools now spends more time assessing teaching and learning earlier in the process to ensure that candidates who reach the final stages of selection have a stronger foundation of teaching and learning. As mentioned previously, **Rice University's Education Entrepreneurship Program** MBA focuses on developing management and operational skills and thus expects its candidates to already be strong in the area of teaching and learning upon admission because there is little training in this area.

> RLA programs construct carefully sequenced and rigorous selection experiences that require candidates to demonstrate their skills and dispositions through real-time performance-based assessments aligned with the required selection criteria.

However, teaching and learning is not a critical selection criterion for all RLA members. **UVA's Partnership for Leaders in Education** program works with school districts to select and prepare turnaround principals. The program uses school turnaround leader competencies developed by Public Impact.[8] Two of the most critical selection criteria are *achievement*, which encompasses belief and driving for results, and *influence*, which captures a person's ability to mobilize and motivate teachers and staff. Because turnaround principals are also likely to be responsible for staff changes and dismissals, the program looks for candidates who are resilient and can handle conflict. Teaching and learning, on the other hand, UVA believes can be further developed through workshops, residencies, and coaching or met through adding strong instructional staff in the school. UVA works with districts and states to develop selection criteria depending on their requirements. In some cases, having a teaching and learning competency intact is not necessarily an upfront requirement.

In another example, **NYC Leadership Academy** seeks applicants who demonstrate professional integrity (as demonstrated by behavior that is consistent with expressed beliefs), a deep commitment to closing the achievement gap, sufficiently developed communication and problem-solving skills, resilience, the capacity to work collaboratively with others, and an openness to the goal of continuous and public learning. When applicants possess these baseline skills and dispositions, the Leadership Academy is able to develop the other school leadership skills necessary to lead school improvement efforts. These include instructional supervision, enhanced communication and problem-solving skills, data analysis, strategic planning, and community engagement.

All of the RLA aspiring principals prepare for positions in urban schools that serve widely diverse student populations. Some RLA programs are considering or already have built into their selection criteria evidence that the candidate can work in diverse school environments. For example, the **University of Illinois at Chicago**, which works closely with Chicago Public Schools, has chosen to articulate *cultural competency* as a critical skill in selection. The program expects candidates to be aware of their own cultural worldview and demonstrate the ability to understand others' perspectives well and to create inclusive environments.

Some RLA programs have differentiated criteria for different types of placement opportunities at the end of the training. The **KIPP School Leadership Program** requires that all school leaders demonstrate *student focus* throughout their professional careers, but they look for different competency strengths for founding school leaders and sustainer/succession school leaders. For founding school leaders, KIPP seeks candidates who are strong in instructional leadership, highly effective at direction-setting, and skillful at communicating with the various stakeholders involved in building a school from the ground up. For sustainer/succession principals, the program looks for individuals who have a strong instructional background, well-established people-management skills, and an ability to manage change successfully in an existing KIPP school.

> Throughout the selection process, RLA organizations are extremely wary of candidates who indicate signs of misalignment with their core beliefs.

Sample Selection Criteria

SELECTION RUBRIC
Based on the KIPP School Leadership Program Framework and Competency Model

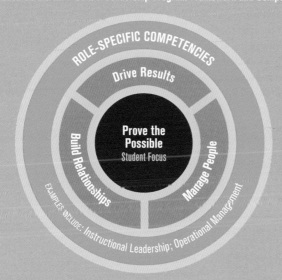

Drive Results
Achievement Orientation
Continuous Learning
Critical Thinking and Problem-solving
Decision Making
Planning and Execution

Build Relationships
Stakeholder Management
Communication
Impact and Influence
Self-awareness
Cultural Competence

Manage People
Direction Setting
Team Leadership
Performance Management
Talent Development

SELECTION CRITERIA
New Leaders for New Schools

Beliefs and Orientation
Belief and Urgency that All
Students Will Excel Academically

Personal Responsibility
and Relentless Drive

Results Orientation

Teaching and Learning
Knowledge of Teaching and Learning

Strategic Management
Problem Solving
Project Management to Deliver Results

Leadership Qualities
Adult Leadership
Communication and Listening
Interpersonal Skills
Self-Awareness and Commitment to Ongoing Learning

More details can be found in Appendix D and online at:
www.nlns.org/Criteria.jsp

TURNAROUND SCHOOL
LEADER COMPETENCIES
UVA's Partnership for Leaders in Education

Driving for Results
Achievement
Initiative and Persistence
Monitoring and Directiveness
Planning Ahead

Influencing for Results
Impact and Influence
Team Leadership
Developing Others

Problem Solving
Analytical Thinking
Conceptual Thinking

Showing Confidence to Lead
Self-Confidence

SOURCE: School Turnaround Leaders: Selection Toolkit
(Public Impact, June 2008), Used by UVA

Designing a Consistent and Fair Selection Process

Once a program is clear about the skills and dispositions it wants candidates to possess upon entry, the next step is determining a consistent and fair process that allows candidates to demonstrate their abilities. At every stage, evidence is collected and assessed against the selection criteria; during some stages candidates may be evaluated on multiple criteria; other stages may focus on a single area, such as teaching and learning. In doing so, the RLA programs amass a significant amount of data on the candidates' skills, knowledge, and dispositions to help them select those with the highest potential for success.

K?

In reading this chapter, you may want to reflect back on these Key Questions to plan your own selection process.

What is the goal of each stage of the selection process—delve deeper into selection criteria already seen or test different criteria? Or both?

What evidence needs to be gathered at each stage? What will applicants be required to submit or to demonstrate in order to elicit that evidence?

How will skills and dispositions be measured? What activities might be used?

RLA members typically define a sequence of single-elimination stages to assess which candidates exhibit the key selection criteria that indicate they could be successful as principals—and thus winnow down their pool of candidates (see the graphic showing the relationship between Recruitment and Selection on page 29). Some RLA programs advance fewer than 50 percent of the applicants after the first stage, enabling subsequent stages to go deeper with fewer candidates.

There is an inherent trade-off in establishing a cut point. While it is more cost efficient to narrow the pool quickly, taking only the obvious top candidates, programs risk passing over talented individuals. On the other hand, programs that retain larger candidate pools through later stages of the process have to expend more resources and sometimes then have to limit their selection activities, risking the opportunity to get an in-depth look at candidates to ensure only the highest-quality ones are selected.

RLA programs vary in the number of stages they use and the activities involved at each stage. They all start with an application (either paper-based or online) that often includes written responses or essays. Most use interviews at some point in the process. Many include a more in-depth experiential event for their highest-potential candidates. The examples in Figure 4 on page 54 are sample sequences from three RLA programs.

As illustrated in the table on page 54, RLA members start with the initial application screen and then construct a series of experiential events to test and unpack candidates' behaviors and responses under a variety of circumstances. What is notable is that while they all use different selection activities and different sequences, every RLA program relies on *evidence-based methods* to assess real-time responses in relation to the selection criteria. The purpose is to test the alignment of applicants' core beliefs against stated values and to bring those beliefs to life through actions. Through a series of multi-dimensional, simulated experiences, the programs gain a deep understanding of how candidates approach and think through challenging situations.

See *Appendix D* for the path to principalship as defined by **Gwinnett County Public Schools**, which includes the application process for the assistant principalship as well as the district's Quality-Plus Leader Academy. Also, the Quality-Plus Leader Academy Leadership Screening Fact Sheet outlines how leadership skills and behaviors are assessed.

SEE PAGE 159

Learn more in Appendix D.

> RLA programs find it is worth investing in a carefully constructed series of activities and experiences designed to elicit multi-faceted evidence consistent with the selection criteria they care most about.

Initial Application Screen

RLA programs typically begin by collecting information relating to the candidate's past experience and work history (résumé, application, written assessments, and references or recommendations). With large numbers of applications, this initial screening process helps programs to narrow the group to those applicants who demonstrate an understanding of the program and overall alignment to the selection criteria.

At this stage, RLA programs often ask candidates to respond to particular questions to assess past performance and learning, personal characteristics and beliefs, interest, and commitment. The purpose of these probing essay questions is to gather evidence of the candidates' skills and dispositions as they relate to the selection criteria. For example, here are some sample essay topics with the related criterion in parentheses:

▶ Why do you want to be an urban school principal? (*belief and results orientation*)

▶ Describe a time when you led students to dramatically improve their results. (*teaching and learning and results orientation*)

▶ Describe a situation where you failed. How did you handle it? What lessons did you learn? (*resilience, self-awareness, and commitment to ongoing learning*)

▶ Describe a situation where you led a team of adults and the high points and low points of that experience. (*adult leadership, results orientation, interpersonal skills, and communication*)

Written essays help the selection team more deeply understand applicants' experiences in responding to difficult situations, their thought processes, and their own self-awareness of their strengths and weaknesses. Essays and written responses are an efficient way for programs to do a first analysis of candidate match to the selection criteria.

Stages of the Selection Process

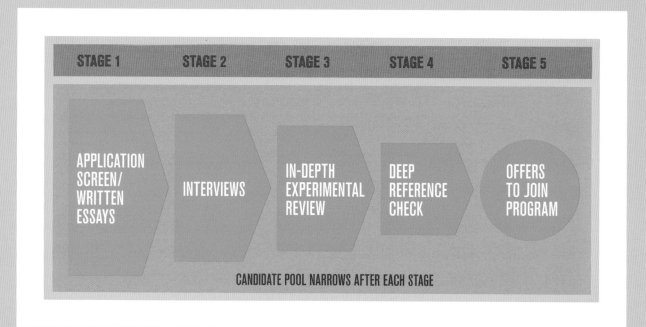

STAGE 1	STAGE 2	STAGE 3	STAGE 4	STAGE 5
APPLICATION SCREEN/ WRITTEN ESSAYS	INTERVIEWS	IN-DEPTH EXPERIMENTAL REVIEW	DEEP REFERENCE CHECK	OFFERS TO JOIN PROGRAM

CANDIDATE POOL NARROWS AFTER EACH STAGE

Sample Selection Sequences

	STAGE 1	STAGE 2	STAGE 3	STAGE 4	STAGE 5
KIPP SCHOOL LEADERSHIP PROGRAM	Online application with essays, résumé, and other biographical information	Phone interview	Videotaped lesson, letters of recommendation, and reference checks	Regional in-person interview and observation of teaching lesson	Three-day selection event
NEW LEADERS FOR NEW SCHOOLS	Online application with essays, résumé, and other biographical information	First-round interview with case presentation and instructional knowledge screen	Finalist Selection Day—full day of experiential exercises	Reference checks	
NYC LEADERSHIP ACADEMY	Online application with essays, résumé, and other biographical information	Facilitated group interview and role-play exercises	Individual instructional interview and review of writing samples/artifacts	Reference checks	

A few programs use commercial assessments to gather information on applicants' knowledge and skill base. For example, **Gwinnett County Public Schools** uses Principal Insight[9] (a Gallup Organization instrument), which it finds to be helpful in uncovering and identifying some soft skills and adult leadership behaviors. For Gwinnett, it is a cost-effective tool for identifying certain selection criteria, such as valuing teamwork over individual leadership, which can sometimes be hard to pick up in other parts of the selection process. Principal Insight scores are only one in a series of data points that Gwinnett uses to assess candidate skills and talents, and the district finds these multiple measures useful in assembling a complete picture.

Based on the information collected as part of this first round of application reviews, RLA selection personnel might only advance as few as half of the applicants (numbers vary by program). This gives them a narrower pool to focus—and expend resources—on during the remaining selection stages.

Real-Time, Experiential Events

In the in-person interviews, RLA members focus on patterns of past behavior (thoughts, actions) and experiential activities that assess their reactions in real time such as simulations, role-plays, and case-study scenarios. RLA programs are looking for a marriage between stated beliefs and skills from the written application and actual behaviors related to the selection criteria. Is the applicant resilient under pressure, and is belief so strong that he or she stays focused on student achievement when there are other competing pressures? Does the applicant show creativity and innovation? Can he or she analyze a problem and construct a solution on the spot? These practical experiential activities about the day-to-day challenges of a school give applicants a chance to demonstrate their leadership qualities. RLA members structure these differently depending on what selection criteria they want to focus on and the staff time and program resources available. The following are some examples:

Instructional Screen. The University of Illinois at Chicago uses an instructional screen to determine a candidate's teaching and learning strengths. Candidates watch a five-minute classroom lesson video, evaluate the quality of instruction and the classroom environment, and propose strategies for the teacher to improve his/her practice. UIC wants to know if candidates know good instruction when they see it. Can they analyze the lesson's quality, including diagnosing strengths and weaknesses? Can they comment on teacher and student engagement? What kinds of feedback would they give to the teacher to improve the lesson? To fare well in the UIC admissions process, candidates must demonstrate their skill through an in-depth discussion about their observations and provide strategies to improve the teaching. (The protocol for the UIC classroom instruction video can be found in *Appendix D.*)

WATCH THE WRITING BIAS

RLA members caution that those who lack an elegant writing style may still possess the skills, knowledge, and dispositions to develop into effective leaders. And the reverse is true as well: Applicants who may be excellent writers with all the right messages are not always the best principal candidates. The programs try to avoid "false negatives"—rejecting those who have less polished writing but offer solid background experience and could have the skills to do the job effectively. Some programs have found that strong writing is often more a product of an individual's quality educational experiences and opportunities (correlated with race and class). Programs are careful not to reject candidates too early in the process based on written material if they otherwise show strong skills and dispositions for the principalship. RLA members read through good but not perfect essays to find the content and substance underneath, as these are the qualities that matter most for the job. This is one reason why RLA members put so much emphasis on experiential interviewing where selectors can see the applicants in action.

Learn more in Appendix D.

SEE PAGE 159

Group Interview. NYC Leadership Academy uses a group interview to assess applicants' problem-solving, communication, self-awareness, and interpersonal skills. In particular, the Leadership Academy seeks to understand how applicants manage ambiguity, respond to challenging situations and setbacks, and relate to others. The Leadership Academy chose to hone in on these particular skills and abilities after reviewing the success of past candidates in the program. Often, those who were unsuccessful and ultimately dismissed from the program lacked the ability to problem-solve and the resilience necessary to bounce back when confronted with tough feedback and challenging situations.

During the Leadership Academy's group interview process, which lasts approximately an hour, applicants review a school leadership scenario that engages them in real-time problem-solving in a fluid context. A Leadership Academy staff member facilitates the group and leads them through a discussion of the scenario using a facilitated conversation protocol. The scenario discussion requires applicants to consider an authentic school dilemma involving issues of school culture and climate, and to demonstrate an awareness of and attention to possible pitfalls and negative responses from various constituent groups. Each applicant responds in the role of the principal during the scenario discussion. The facilitator gives individual applicants coaching tips to see how quickly they can accommodate and respond to feedback and to assess their resilience. After applicants respond to the scenario, the facilitator changes the circumstances presented in the scenario to see how applicants adjust to a changed context, assess their ability to problem-solve effectively under changed circumstances, and observe whether they consider unintended consequences. Throughout the group interview, the facilitator probes applicants' values, encourages them to work as a team, and pushes them to think through implementation challenges and the implications of their proposed actions. This process enables the Leadership Academy to obtain good information about each applicant's ability to analyze causation and develop a strategic plan. (See *Appendix D* for a sample of a NYC Leadership Academy facilitated group interview.)

SEE PAGE 159

Learn more in Appendix D.

Behavioral-Event Interview. The University of Virginia's Partnership for Leaders in Education (PLE) program helps districts identify strong candidates to lead turnaround schools. PLE puts a lot of weight on its behavioral-event interview during which candidates describe in detail one example of a successful event and one example of an event in which they failed or were frustrated. These two open-ended yet focused interviews ask candidates to describe concretely what they did, said, thought, and felt during the events, giving interviewers a clear picture of how candidates approached each situation and their rationale for their actions. The selectors are trained to elicit the appropriate depth of information so they can score for competencies and characteristics based on the evidence provided. Information obtained via these interviews is considered in conjunction with the candidate's experience, past performance, credentials, etc.

SUPPORT CANDIDATES' SELF REFLECTION

RLA programs, by and large, place a lot of importance on self-awareness and continuous learning as selection criteria, seeing them as prerequisites to the rapid learning necessary to prepare for the principalship in a year. However, candidates, used to traditional interview settings, often come in focused on selling themselves and their abilities. What is different about RLA methods is that they actually want applicants to self-assess, be reflective, and share weaknesses during the interview process. This is a departure from what many expect in an interview and a cultural shift for many who have been taught to present confidence; thus, RLA programs think carefully about how to draw people out. They have found that it helps to be very upfront about the purpose of these conversations and to share with candidates that their selection processes are nontraditional and require honest reflection. It is also helpful to assure candidates that their assessment of another candidate's engagement during any group activity is only used to understand their thinking, not to measure that candidate in the process. RLA programs also consciously try to create a safe environment for people to share their mistakes and identify areas that need further growth and development.

> Even programs with the most rigorous selection processes make selection mistakes that require fellows to be dismissed or counseled out of the program. RLA programs review the profiles of the unsuccessful candidates to try to learn from their mistakes and refine the selection process.

Presentation. To test the readiness of candidates to take on leadership positions in Chicago Public Schools, the **University of Illinois at Chicago** has applicants prepare a strategy for turning around a failing Chicago school, which they present to a panel of selectors. Using either a grammar school or a high school case study, candidates are expected to make a presentation on their strategy to turn around the school within three years. The presentation is followed by an intense question-and-answer period during which the candidate is expected to defend his/her school plan to simulate the pressures of the principalship. This exercise is demanding and comprehensive, assessing multiple candidate qualities across multiple domains. Three that are particularly salient are that the candidate: 1) displays the analytic abilities, skills, and dispositions to gather critical information and strategically analyze it; 2) displays the experience, maturity, and communication and self-presentation skills likely to win the confidence and cooperation of staff, local school council, and community stakeholders; and 3) shows awareness of, and dispositions toward, what we know about effective practices in transformational leadership. (A copy of the UIC interview schedule can be found in *Appendix D.*)

SEE PAGE 159

Learn more in Appendix D.

Finalist Selection Day. The **KIPP School Leadership Program** hosts a three-day finalist selection event for its highest-potential candidates. During the event, candidates participate in four one-hour interviews with a team of two senior leaders from across the KIPP network. (These senior leaders represent high-performing current KIPP school leaders and regional leaders who formerly founded and led high-performing KIPP schools.) These selector teams assess a variety of KIPP competencies in order to understand how a candidate thinks about instructional excellence, organizational performance, and individual strengths and weaknesses as a leader. KIPP employs an experiential approach, asking candidates to share past experiences and probing for details on their actions, thoughts, and reflections following the experience. Selectors also test candidates on the spot by presenting a specific challenging school-based situation (e.g., a challenging meeting with a member of the school community, an end-of-the-year data review with staff members) and asking them to role-play their response so the selectors can see how the candidate handles the simulated situation. The interviews are standardized and consistent, and the selectors use interview guides and group norms that are very intentionally built to ensure that the process is evidence-based and that the selector teams are focused on the selection criteria.

Even though multiple behavior-based methods require a lot of program staff time, RLA programs value the real-time information gained in contrast with the more traditional paper-based application processes that focus solely on past experience. RLA programs find it is worth investing in a carefully constructed series of activities and experiences designed to elicit multi-faceted evidence consistent with the selection criteria they care most about.

Executing a Fair and Consistent Process

After designing a rigorous process, RLA programs strive to ensure that the process is implemented fairly and all candidates are given the same opportunities to demonstrate their skills and behaviors. First, they create a variety of appropriate evaluation instruments and then they prepare their selectors to use those instruments in a consistent fashion.

> How will you ensure an objective process? What rubrics, guides, or instruments might you create to undergird the process for consistency?

> Who from the program will be involved in the selection process? Will additional external people be part of the selection process?

> How will you ensure that selection committee members are knowledgeable about the program and the selection criteria to determine which candidates would be a good fit? How will you ensure that the criteria are normalized to provide consistent and accurate assessments?

> How will you ensure that the selection process discussions and evaluations of candidates are kept confidential?

Tools and Instruments

RLA programs use a robust set of tools to compile a complete picture of a candidate's strengths and weaknesses in relation to the selection criteria. Various instruments help them to increase objectivity as well as making sure that the process runs smoothly. These include:

Interview Guides. Interview guides help clarify key questions and possible probes based on candidates' responses so that interviews are conducted consistently, allowing every applicant the same opportunities to demonstrate their abilities and discuss their experiences. Some RLA members use interview scripts, have sample questions to probe for more information, and use templates to capture interview notes. While the interview guides ensure a consistent approach, some programs allow selectors to veer from the script when they want to probe for greater depth and collect more information from a candidate in order to be able to evaluate them accurately against the selection criteria.

Rubrics. Evaluation rubrics (ideally, for each stage of the selection process) are extremely helpful in ensuring that multiple evaluators are rating applicants based on a common scoring system on each selection criterion. Again, this ensures consistency of candidate evaluation and also provides a quantitative measure that can be compared down the road as candidates progress through the development process and matriculate. (See the **New Leaders for New Schools** selection criteria rubric sample and the **University of Virginia's Partnership for Leaders in Education** competency scoring sample in *Appendix D.*)

SEE PAGE 159

Learn more in
Appendix D.

Selection Matrices. A selection matrix maps the selection process activities and submissions in relation to the selection criteria so that selectors know when the candidates have opportunities to demonstrate their skills and dispositions. Ideally, candidates will have multiple opportunities to address each of the criteria. The matrix is then used as an evaluator's tool to help selectors compile a composite score in each area. The matrix can also be used as a training tool for selection personnel to help them understand where they are to look for certain skills and dispositions. Ultimately, this makes selectors more effective because they feel empowered to focus on specific areas of a larger selection model, and they do not feel obligated to gather evidence of every selection competency in one interaction. (See a Sample Selection Matrix in *Appendix D.*)

SEE PAGE 159

Learn more in
Appendix D.

AWARENESS OF POTENTIAL BIASES

RLA programs caution that selectors may bring an unconscious bias (positive or negative) to the table. Biases may be for certain types of people or for certain organizations or associations. These may be hard for selectors to acknowledge automatically and need to be pulled out through effective pre-selection facilitated discussions with selectors. Some programs use role-play scenarios to help selectors to be aware of their automatic first impressions when interviewing a candidate who is well-dressed and very polished as compared to a candidate who speaks with a foreign accent or uses a less formal presentation style.

Selectors

Tools are a very important part of the process in that they promote a uniform and objective approach to selection. However, the people who use the various tools and instruments are just as important. RLA programs think carefully about their selectors and recognize that they need training and support in order to use the instruments consistently. Because RLA programs use multiple sources of information and draw from numerous experiences and performances, it can be difficult to ensure inter-rater overall objectivity and uniformity. To help ensure a common and coherent approach to scoring applicants, RLA programs typically provide some training on calibration and take time to establish norms among the selector group.

One way of training selectors is by conducting mock selection events together. For instance, different selectors might practice interviewing the same candidate and rating the candidate's performance using a rubric. The interviewers then meet to share their rubric ratings and discuss scoring similarities and differences. Where there is divergent thinking, selectors discuss their perspectives and come to agreement on the appropriate rating. Similar calibration processes can be conducted using a mock candidate's résumé, application, and essays. The selectors also might watch video role-plays, discuss as a group, and calibrate their scores based on what they observed.

The University of Virginia's Partnership for Leaders in Education (PLE) uses a two-day training program to prepare its assessors to facilitate behavioral-event interviews (described above) and score candidates. The first day focuses on interviewing skills and how to guide candidates to the level of detail required so that they have sufficient opportunity to address each of the 10 competencies. Participants learn the model, watch a mini-example, practice with colleagues, get feedback on their interviewing skills, and give feedback to others in their group. The topic of the second day is using competency data, scoring, and calibration. UVA uses a very rigorous process that allows only information and evidence shared during the behavioral-event interview to be considered in the scores (no outside information). UVA not only trains its partner-district or state assessors but also conducts a model selection session at least once before setting the program off on its own to select.

Using Selection Data to Make Decisions and Inform Participants' Development

During the selection process, RLA programs construct extremely robust profiles of each applicant. The various stages of paper review, interviewing, and real-time experiential events result in a massive and comprehensive body of data that RLA programs are careful to catalog.

Scoring techniques vary by program but RLA members typically set a minimum bar that a candidate must reach in order to be selected. A candidate may need to reach a minimum total score or a certain minimum score on each selection criteria. Some criteria may be weighted more heavily than others. This, again, relates to program policies about having certain selection criteria relatively secure upon admission versus those that can be more easily or cost-effectively trained for during the development period. Establishing an objective, evidence-based decision point allows for a transparent selection process. Data generated during selection are used in various ways:

1. Selection Decisions
Using the information gathered across the various stages of the selection process, selection personnel make decisions about each candidate. RLA programs often group their candidates into three categories:

▷ **Accept.** This candidate demonstrated enough knowledge, skills, and dispositions against the selection criteria throughout the process, and the program is ready to accept this individual into the program. Program leaders have confidence that they can train this individual in all areas of the Competency Framework that the candidate did not demonstrate proficiency in during selection.

DETERMINING WHAT INFORMATION TO CONSIDER IN SELECTION

One issue that RLA members have had to address in the evaluation process is the inclusion of information gathered outside the selection process (for example, personal interactions, gossip, matters of public record, etc.). Most have chosen to rely primarily on the information generated from the selection process including references; however, if an organization has direct, demonstrable evidence of past performance within a similar setting, they may weigh the benefits and costs of integrating that evidence into an assessment of a candidate. For instance, an organization like **KIPP**, where candidates may have grown professionally within their network, might use input from a former regional manager as one element of their candidate assessment. Given that the KIPP School Leadership Program has internal pipeline development pathways, the program may have more direct evidence of candidates' historical performance that can be incorporated into their selection reviews. **New Leaders for New Schools** is beginning to think through how it can make use of information collected in recruiting. At this point, recruitment evaluations are not used in selection, but the program is considering melding recruitment and pipeline program information for selection data.

▷ **Deny, but designate as an "Aspiring Leader."** This candidate showed strong potential and scored well on some criteria, but is not ready for admission into the program. RLA members, very cognizant of building a pipeline of future candidates, let the individual know that the program has interest in having them apply again. Based on their scores on specific criteria during the selection process, RLA programs provide feedback on areas to improve and how the candidate might address them before the next application period. Some programs work directly with these potential candidates on their development. While not a guarantee of future admission, this keeps candidates connected to the program.

▷ **Deny.** This candidate is not ready for the program, nor does the program estimate that the candidate will be ready in the next few years.

Within their program design, some RLA programs have defined different pathways that provide various intensities of training. For example, **KIPP**'s Fisher Fellowship is a one-year pathway to founding a new KIPP school. The Miles Family Fellowship is a two-year pathway for founding and leading a new KIPP school. By having these two options, KIPP can identify various "runways" for leadership. While some candidates may not be ready for the one-year Fisher Fellowship, KIPP's two-year option may be an appropriate fit.

EXAMPLE

2. Individual Learning Plans

The selection data and ratings not only determine which candidates are accepted into the program, but also serve as inputs to Individual Learning Plans (ILPs) and customized supports for their new program matriculants. RLA programs compile the data collected during the various selection stages and devise customized plans for the entrants to ensure that they get the support needed to progress at a fast rate while in the program. ILPs are shared with the program staff handling training and development to ensure a smooth transition and flow of information. This information is then used with the matriculating participant in the co-creation of the ILP. (This topic is covered in more depth in the *Training and Developing Fellows* chapter.)

SELECTOR PREPARATION IS CRITICAL

A note of caution: Training selection committee members can be time-consuming and may require significant planning. RLA members warn that even with the best-designed process, execution by the selectors is crucial. Without a normed process, there is a risk that Selector A and Selector B may hear the same information but score a candidate very differently on assessment tools. Programs need to train selectors and give them time to establish common practices and scoring methods. Begin planning this activity early in the year.

SEE PAGE 68

Learn more in the Training and Developing Fellows chapter.

Evaluation and Assessment of the Selection Process

Data collected are also used to construct a long-term feedback loop for RLA programs, helping them to improve their efficacy and overall success in predicting which applicants will become effective principals. Some of the key questions that RLA programs consider when constructing their databases are listed on page 62.

Even programs with the most rigorous selection processes make selection mistakes that require fellows to be dismissed or counseled out of the program. RLA programs review the profiles of the unsuccessful candidates to try to learn from their mistakes and refine the selection process.

K?

In reading this chapter, you may want to reflect back on these Key Questions to plan your own selection process.

> How will your evaluation system capture variations in qualities among successful candidates, not just between successful and unsuccessful candidates?
>
> How will you continuously monitor fellows (some of whom ultimately may not make it to the principalship) to learn about key strengths/weaknesses that may be related to later success?
>
> How will you balance the program's interest in having a consistent tool for measuring long-term impacts with the need to adapt data-gathering tools to reflect the inevitable modifications to the design (as part of continuous improvement)?

RLA programs also monitor the performance of their graduates on the job after program completion. They correlate their effectiveness as principals with their selection process ratings to strengthen their selection criteria and overall process for finding and securing high-potential candidates. To do this well, programs need to have rubrics and other evaluation tools that have enough nuance and detail from which they can draw solid conclusions. Just using a four-point scale on the selection criteria, for example, may not provide the variability and depth of information needed to help programs discern why some successful applicants—all of whom were highly rated in order to be accepted—were more successful than others once they reached their school sites. By changing the tool used to measure selection competencies, programs may be able to better link outcomes to inputs (skills, knowledge, and dispositions) on the front end. However, RLA members caution that if assessment tools change too frequently, programs lose the ability to evaluate their effectiveness from year to year. Programs feel this constant tension between the need to make adjustments to their design based on short-term results and the interest in having consistent evaluative tools to allow them to collect long-term data on the effectiveness of their program.

SELECTION CRITERIA MINIMUMS

New Leaders for New Schools uses a 1-to-4 rating scale, with 4 being the highest score on each selection criteria. Belief is the most important to New Leaders for New Schools and applicants are required to score a 4 to be admitted to the program. Applicants need to score a minimum of 3 in the other areas.

COST AND RESOURCE ALLOCATION CONSIDERATIONS

A rigorous selection process can be very resource-and staff-intensive. RLA programs have chosen to invest in experiential events to help them identify the strongest candidates. But they recognize that these in-person interviews and simulations require a lot of program staff time. There are onetime initial development costs to create tools and instruments that help ensure a consistent and fair process. There are also ongoing staff costs involved in preparing the selectors to use the tools effectively and from time-to-time to update the tools with new learning from the performance of program graduates. Program staff must conduct the initial application screen and plan for and implement the real-time experiential events. There may be travel costs involved as well for staff or candidates. For the RLA members, this large upfront investment of human capital is necessary to select and admit a strong cohort.

Programs are challenged to find the right distribution of resources among recruitment, selection, training, and support. If there is a greater investment upfront to identify and select a small group of really strong aspiring principals, the costs involved in developing that cohort may be smaller. However, this approach risks passing over candidates who have the potential to be very effective principals with the right training and supports. RLA members caution that these decisions cannot be made with a simple calculation. Each program has to find a balance that works in the context of the districts and schools it serves, and within resource constraints. Changes may be made year to year depending on program circumstances.

Lessons Learned

RLA programs all agree that a rigorous selection process is an essential component of a successful principal preparation program. RLA programs have invested enormous resources to ensure that they:

1. Select candidates who have competencies that they believe are critical to success but may be difficult to teach or train for in the allotted time period.

2. Provide applicants numerous opportunities to demonstrate their skills and abilities through experiential activities. Selection events simulate consequential decision-making with changing circumstances to test candidates' beliefs and consistency of behaviors. RLA members value these experiential events as they shed light in a way that paper-based applications cannot on a candidate's ability to think fast, analyze problems, and design solutions that adhere to their core beliefs.

3. Use a transparent selection process that ensures consistent assessment of the selection criteria. RLA programs employ a variety of tools and instruments to compile as complete and accurate a picture of candidates' strengths and weaknesses as possible.

4. Train and norm selectors. The selection process is only as good as the people involved in making the selection decisions. Take the time to prepare your selectors, give them time together to practice and discuss scoring issues to ensure a calibrated and objective process.

5. Catalog and analyze the range of data gathered during the selection process for the benefit of individual applicants as they move into the program for training and development, pipeline development, and continuous improvement of the program.

A Look Ahead: Training and Developing Fellows

Once fellows are selected, programs turn their attention to designing a sequence of training and development experiences to prepare them for effective school leadership. This next chapter delves into RLA approaches to coursework, the residency experience, and coaching.

Training and Developing Fellows

CONTINUUM OF PRINCIPAL PREPARATION

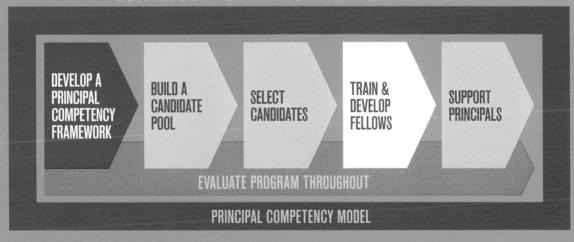

DEVELOP A PRINCIPAL COMPETENCY FRAMEWORK

BUILD A CANDIDATE POOL

SELECT CANDIDATES

TRAIN & DEVELOP FELLOWS

SUPPORT PRINCIPALS

EVALUATE PROGRAM THROUGHOUT

PRINCIPAL COMPETENCY MODEL

4 TRAINING AND DEVELOPING FELLOWS | RLA programs believe that *training and development needs to be school-based and experiential.* Each fellow has an Individual Learning Plan that takes into account strengths and weaknesses identified during the selection process. The development sequences are intentionally coordinated and integrated and include coursework and school-based residencies that give fellows authentic opportunities to lead adults, make mistakes, and grow. Additionally, throughout the process, fellows are given feedback and provided on-going coaching. For RLA programs, coaching is not about the role of the coach but is an action and a strategy for providing regular, constructive, and critical feedback. If during the course of the training and development period, a fellow does not demonstrate the rate of growth or the skill sets needed to be successful on the job, RLA programs are willing to dismiss the individual from the

The Training and Development Process

program. While de-selection is not commonplace, RLA programs are clear that their purpose is to prepare effective principals on behalf of students.

After selecting a new cohort, most RLA principal preparation and development programs typically have a year to 18 months to prepare their fellows to assume school leadership positions. While the programs take a variety of approaches to training and development, they all use their Competency Frameworks to map out a series of aligned activities to prepare fellows with the essential skills, knowledge, and dispositions needed for effective school leadership. (As discussed in previous chapters, those competencies that are not well established upon admission to the program need to be addressed through training and development.)

Learn more in previous chapters.

RLA members use all of the information they have on fellows (selection information, self-assessments, early observations) to target the learning needs of each individual. "Training and development" encompasses coursework, experiential in-school practice, and some form of ongoing feedback or coaching to ensure that fellows develop and hone their skills quickly and effectively. Throughout, RLA programs draw on not only the expertise of their networks of practitioners, expert faculty, and program staff, but also the power of the cohort of peers within the program to help fellows stay on a steep learning curve.

> For RLA programs, coaching is not about the role of the coach but is an action and a strategy for providing regular, constructive, and critical feedback.

Individual Learning Plans

RLA programs immediately put to use information gathered about fellows during the selection process to pinpoint areas where further development and experience are needed. While fellows are expected to enter the program with many competencies at least somewhat established, each fellow will have areas of relative weakness that the program focuses on for development. (Most programs reinforce to some degree all the competencies.) Independent data from observations and selection are combined and calibrated with the individual's self-assessment of strengths and areas of growth. Program staff and the fellow collaborate to craft development goals and Individual Learning Plans (ILPs). This ensures ownership from the fellow and a common understanding of the underlying objectives of each of the training and development experiences. RLA programs that prepare principals for various school settings (charter, turnaround, start-up, etc.) adjust ILPs to account for likely placements upon graduation. They are careful to tailor the experiential work/residency to match the fellow with an appropriate school and school leader who can mentor in the needed growth areas.

How will the Competency Framework be used to target and guide specific learning to meet each fellow's needs?

What is the right balance of coursework, experiential learning, and targeted feedback to develop an effective principal? How can development activities be *customized* to meet individual needs?

How will you make *coursework meaningful* so that it prepares an aspiring principal to do the job instead of merely knowing the theory behind it?

How will fellows be given authentic, real-life experiences that allow them to *practice* the things they are learning? How will they get to *see strong leaders* in action?

How will fellows have the opportunity to *assume real leadership of adults* and have the space to practice and make mistakes?

How will fellows get ongoing *feedback* throughout the development process?

What will be the role of faculty, coaches, mentor-principals, peers, and others in developing each fellow, and how will all of these people *communicate and coordinate*?

What *resources* (time, talented people, effective school models, money) do you have or need for fellow development, and thus what are your limitations?

How will fellows be assessed during the program and at the conclusion of their training and development experiences?

NYC Leadership Academy creates an ILP known as the Compact, which has two components: 1) *general expectations* that all participants are expected to complete during the program, such as participating in learning walks, supervising teachers, administering school quality reviews; and 2) *targeted practice areas* that address individual growth areas with specific practice activities to enhance skills. For example, if a participant has weak communication skills, he or she might be required to plan and lead a series of activities to build skills in this area, such as team and committee meetings and parent-teacher conferences. Participants who struggle with resiliency might be asked to deliver a full professional development sequence to a group of resistant teachers. These multiple practice sessions allow participants to get feedback and hone their skills until they are comfortable and proficient. The Compact is viewed as a living, dynamic document that gets adjusted as needed to ensure that the participant is on track to demonstrate all of the required competencies upon graduation. (A sample Compact can be found in *Appendix E.*)

By generating ILPs upfront, the fellow and those who come into contact with him/her throughout the program (program leadership, faculty, coaches, mentor-principals, etc.) have a clear understanding of and can assertively target development goals and the activities and experiences necessary to help the fellow be ready for a principalship. The ILP is not simply put aside but is revisited throughout the development phase as a reflection, feedback, and monitoring tool. The program also uses it to make good matches to mentor-principals, coaches, and residency placement, and ultimately to evaluate the overall progress and readiness of the fellow relative to the Competency Framework. (See *Appendix E* for a summary of the **New Leaders for New Schools** Individual Learning Plan template.)

SEE PAGE 172

Learn more
in Appendix E.

Training and Development Goals and Delivery

Training and development experiences are sequenced to build readiness for a principalship upon program completion. Personalizing the development experiences to focus on individual learning goals and objectives is important. RLA members believe deeply in giving fellows hands-on, experiential learning scenarios that challenge them to respond to the kinds of complex situations that are common in a real urban school principalship.

RLA programs typically have three training and development components: coursework, a residency (or other experiential component), and coaching (or other ongoing feedback mechanism).

As indicated in the diagram on page 71, these three main elements are interrelated, interdependent, and must be closely aligned. Communication between the people responsible for each of the different elements is important, as is constant feedback to the fellow to target growth areas and support learning.

RLA programs note the importance of considering the context of the program and the future schools where fellows will serve as principals, which influence the structure and design of training and development. Variables include:

▷ Depth of experience of fellows before they enter the program
▷ Coordination and cohesiveness of district or CMO operations and management
▷ Types of schools fellows will serve in as future principals
▷ Duration of the program and resources available for training and development

Coursework, *residency*, and *coaching* are each defined and discussed in the diagram on the following page.

Training and Development Components

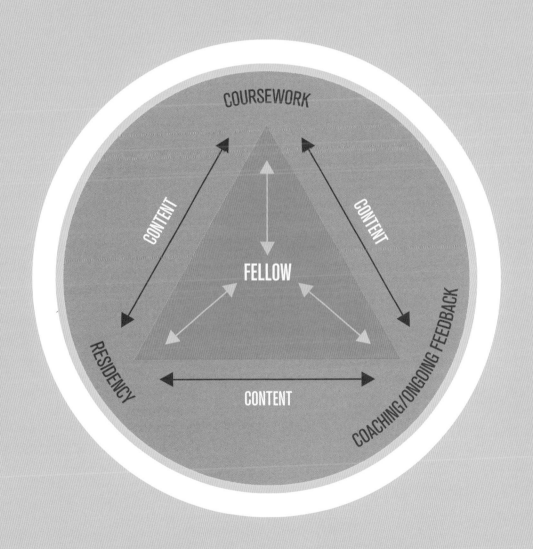

Coursework

RLA programs usually begin by immersing fellows in coursework. Courses are aligned to the Competency Framework criteria to ensure that they teach fellows the skills and dispositions needed to be effective as a principal.

Delivery Approach

RLA programs ground their coursework in theory but recognize that the principalship is action-based. These programs feel strongly that merely reading, thinking, discussing, or writing about how to approach situations will not allow the fellow to fully integrate the learning. They depart from the more traditional, instructor-focused principal preparation method, using instead a workshop model where the fellows practice and live the lessons as much as possible through role-plays, case studies, simulations, team activities, etc. Fellows with varying backgrounds and growth areas benefit from the projects and group work that promote peer learning and interaction.

EXAMPLE Even RLA programs that are university-based, such as the **University of Illinois at Chicago**, have moved away from courses that teach solely theory. UIC has pushed university faculty to design courses in ways that introduce relevant theory and force students to grapple with theory in real-world, application-oriented activities. Students are expected to collect and analyze extensive data from their existing jobs and/or residency sites. Real schools, teachers, and students are the context for classroom learning experiences.

In addition, faculty members are always grounding the coursework in real-life situations. For example, fellows might read a case that includes second-grade test data and be asked to work as part of a teacher team to analyze the data and devise a plan of action. Fellows are assigned different roles on the team (such as a resistant teacher, an eager teacher, and a struggling teacher). The group models a real-life situation and fellows take turns leading the team discussion. Faculty, and other fellows, observe the conversation and give feedback. Afterward, the group discusses and evaluates the overall process, how they felt in the different roles, etc. The exercise is then repeated with other participants role-playing so that the group can see different styles and approaches at work. These simulated real-life leadership experiences and practice sessions give them a chance to apply their learning and build their skills before they have to do it with real teacher teams during the residency period.

UIC strives to achieve a balance between professor-led and practice-oriented authentic activities.

Scaffolded learning experiences are important to build readiness for resident work and for later academic courses and tasks. The goal is to simulate real-life situations while in the classroom as practice prior to moving into a school-based residency, where fellows practice through real (though supervised) situations in which they are expected to make a positive impact. The classroom experiences provide a safe space to make mistakes and continue to develop.

Delivery Model

Most of the RLA programs, but not all, utilize a "summer intensive" model, conducting the bulk of the classroom workshop learning and

>
> RLA members believe deeply in giving fellows hands-on, experiential learning scenarios that challenge them to respond to the kinds of complex situations that are common in real urban school principalships.

How is the theory connected to application in actual school-based situations? How much theory is necessary?

How is effective leadership modeled as you deliver coursework? How will fellows get to practice the work in the courses and scaffold their learning? What delivery mechanisms are most effective and when?

Who will facilitate and teach the material? Will you use instructors internal or external to your program, or a combination?

How will lessons be differentiated to match the different development needs of fellows?

How will your fellows get a credential, assuming they need one? (e.g., university partnership? Alternative certification route for your program?)

Who will oversee the curriculum to ensure that it is aligned to the Competency Framework, that each module fits into the whole, and that all of the other programmatic elements are aligned effectively?

K?

In reading this chapter, you may want to consider these Key Questions as you plan your training and development strategy.

theory work in the summer (ranging from two to six weeks) prior to entering the residency. This approach helps the fellow to make the transition in perspective from "teacher" to "leader" and provides a foundation of understanding for the individual to start the residency in addition to providing an opportunity to build a strong, unified cohort. In several cases, the summer coursework is centered on a simulated authentic experience. Several RLA programs use a detailed, data-rich case of a school to which fellows apply all of their learning through simulations: role-plays, major analyses, decisions, and presentations.

Many RLA programs continue to provide fellows with coursework during their experiential learning component. Some offer half-day or full-day trainings or workshops with some frequency (weekly, biweekly, monthly). Others plan intensive multiple-day intersessions or quarterly workshops during the training year. These sessions introduce new material that fellows are just ready for, or apply learning to situations they have encountered during their residency. They also allow fellows to meet and share experiences.

RLA programs vary in the time devoted to coursework and who teaches it. The chart on page 74 provides some sample coursework delivery structures.

Coursework Delivery Structure

PROGRAM	TIME ALLOTTED FOR COURSEWORK	FACULTY
GWINNETT COUNTY PUBLIC SCHOOLS (aspiring principals)	12 one-day sessions	Mainly internal to district, including instruction by superintendent
KIPP (FISHER FELLOWS) (aspiring principals)	5 week Summer Institute; 2 one-week Intersessions; 1 two-week Intersession; and 1 long-weekend retreat	Largely external experts and some internal instructors; combination of practitioners and non-practitioners
NEW LEADERS FOR NEW SCHOOLS (aspiring principals)	4 weeks over summer; 2 one-week national sessions; 2 one-week regional sessions; weekly day-long workshops	Largely external experts and some internal instructors; combination of practitioners and non-practitioners
NYC LEADERSHIP ACADEMY (aspiring principals)	6 weeks in the summer; 1.5 days a week during residency	Full-time program staff; program facilitators (faculty) are experienced practitioners who design curriculum, serve as classroom instructors and coaches for participants
UNIVERSITY OF ILLINOIS AT CHICAGO (aspiring and practicing principals)	3 years + a capstone experience (Ph.D. program)	UIC professors, sometimes paired with experts or practitioners

Courses are aligned to the Competency Framework criteria to ensure that they teach fellows the skills and dispositions needed to be effective as a principal.

As evident in the chart at left, program context matters. For instance, **Gwinnett County** draws the majority of its aspiring principals from its own schools, and in many cases the fellows have been in the leadership development pipeline for years. This prior experience base means fellows often know each other coming in, are familiar with school challenges, are grounded in the district culture, and have received much prior training. For this reason, the program devotes less time to coursework than other programs do. **New Leaders for New Schools**, on the other hand, selects its fellows from a much broader pool of applicants from around the country. The program begins with a powerful training experience to build trust and relationships and to immerse the fellows in the "New Leaders for New Schools" way. The **University of Illinois at Chicago** is an intense, doctoral program with three years of coursework and a one-year capstone experience.

Role of Faculty and Other Experts

RLA programs are very concerned about the quality of the curriculum and the people who deliver it. The chart on page 74 shows the variations between programs. While **Gwinnett County** relies almost entirely on internal district staff to teach its courses, **KIPP School Leadership Program** and **New Leaders for New Schools** draw mostly on external experts from across the country and their own high-performing principal practitioners.

Other RLA programs engage their client districts/CMOs and practitioners to develop and deliver some coursework to bring relevant context and draw on local expertise. For example, RLA programs might choose to:

▷ Collaborate with the *target district and/or CMO* to ensure that the curriculum design is most relevant for fellows as they enter the principalship in that particular context.

▷ Call on experienced, highly effective *principals* (often their alums) to deliver the coursework as they offer a credible voice and perspective and can draw on their practical experience. RLA programs try to find principals who have expertise in a certain area (e.g., data-driven instruction, instructional supervision, change management, budget) and can bring real-life experiences to their teaching.

▷ Take advantage of the knowledge base and expertise housed within their *staff,* including coaches, and their alumni to design and deliver curriculum

▷ Engage *national experts* who specialize in and are extremely knowledgeable about certain topic areas. These experts are often called in to help RLA programs design and deliver curriculum, providing best-in-class relevant material and offering a fresh perspective about what it takes to drive dramatic improvement in schools. They might also conduct train-the-trainer workshops to share their content knowledge, skills, and expertise with staff, coaches, and local principals.

Whether or not they engage outside experts and practitioners, RLA programs contend that the best way to teach fellows is through example—and thus they create opportunities to model quality instruction and they mix direct delivery with experiential opportunity.

Content

RLA programs align the content of their coursework to their Competency Frameworks. This coherence is important to make sure that fellows are prepared with the range of skills, knowledge, and dispositions they need to be effective on the job. Within each course, programs map out the learning objectives and incorporate a sequence of increasingly challenging activities and experiential events to build participants' capacity. (See *Appendix E* for segments of the **NYC Leadership Academy's** Aspiring Principals Program summer-intensive themes and summer-intensive sample days, as well as the **New Leaders for New Schools'** foundational-year scope and sequence.)

SEE PAGE 172

Learn more in Appendix E.

RLA member programs agree that the following areas are key topics to cover in coursework:

- Cultural Competency
- Facilitation and Communication Skills—Internal and External (public relations, building relationships with the staff, community leadership, building a community base)
- High Expectations Culture (culture of efficacy, high expectations for all)
- Innovation and Change Management (not accepting the status quo; working for systems change as necessary)
- Instructional Leadership
- Operational Management (business, facilities, budget)
- Organizational Leadership (defining and matching budget, systems, and structures to mission, vision, values)
- People Leadership/ Human Capital Management and Development (teacher and leader capacity development and accountability)
- Personal Leadership (self-awareness, resilience, ethics and integrity, strategic thinking/judgment)
- Systems Thinking (includes comprehensive school diagnosis and action planning)
- Using Data to Improve Teaching and Learning

EXAMPLE

New Leaders for New Schools, like other RLA programs, revamps and revises its curriculum on a regular basis based on feedback from participants, faculty, and coaches as well as survey and observational data linked to the performance of their first- through fifth-year principals. For example, after finding that principals did not know well enough how to shape school culture beyond implementing a discipline system, the program revisited its school culture course. Fellows are now taught concrete, actionable steps to implement on day one, week one, month one and so on to build a positive school climate. Program participants are already much more explicitly focused on setting high expectations, building culture, collecting evidence, and monitoring school culture indicators in their schools.

At different stages of the year, fellows are ready to integrate different depths of understanding of certain topics, and so it becomes necessary to revisit them with deeper levels of complexity. RLA programs have a transparent scope and sequence with critical elements of the curriculum spiraling throughout. A couple of curriculum pieces that some RLA programs revisit and deepen throughout the year are: 1) teaching and learning, specifically observation and supervision; and 2) data-driven instruction.

ADMINISTRATIVE CREDENTIALS

RLA programs determine what sort of partnerships they need to ensure that their fellows get the administrative credentials required by the state. Some programs require fellows to have their credentials before entering the program; others are authorized as alternative credential programs or are universities with regular credential pathways; and others partner with universities for the credit while still ensuring that the program retains the ability to deliver its own content.

When a university partner is needed for certification purposes, RLA programs are sure to attend upfront to issues of cost sharing, faculty decisions, and time commitment of busy fellows to avoid duplicating training work or topics, and to ensure that faculty understand application of theory to practice. Also, if partnering with a university, programs consider whether this precludes working with faculty from other universities. Some university partners agree to review the program curriculum and then give credit for program coursework, without requiring fellows to enroll in university classes. Here, their role is oversight and sign-off on the quality of the program.

For the **University of Illinois at Chicago**, instructional leadership is one of the 12 key Success Factors on the Chicago Public Schools Competency Framework (used as UIC's Competency Framework for the first 18 months of the program). Instructional leadership is first introduced with an overview and an overarching framework so that students come to understand the range of leadership considerations and actions that are associated with the competency of instructional leadership. As the curriculum goes deeper, fellows are introduced to and expected to develop expertise with one classroom observational tool. The initial focus is on developing expertise in recognizing and documenting particular classroom behaviors and practices. Later, UIC adds content-specific observational tools and introduces more detailed pre- and post-conferencing strategies. This scaffolded approach helps aspiring principals build their knowledge base and gives them high-quality tools, which they can then use in their schools. The fellows practice at each interval with the new tools and build them into their repertoire.

RLA programs stress the importance of having a coherent and cohesive curriculum that effectively organizes and integrates central ideas so fellows can see how the ideas build on or connect with other ideas, enabling them to develop new understandings and skills.

The **KIPP School Leadership Program** has recognized the importance of coherence and cohesion in its coursework. In Spring 2010, in anticipation of the summer and year, the program held a faculty symposium, which brought together faculty (experts who generally teach specific modules, as well as full-time staff) from all over the country to illustrate connections between the various courses and their fit within a larger scope and sequence. The symposium served many purposes:

▷ Strengthening awareness of the Summer Institute goals, the Competency Framework, and the urgency around improving participant, and thus, student outcomes
▷ Providing instructors the opportunity to engage with fellow faculty to discuss and make connections among their course content and goals
▷ Providing professional development regarding adult learning strategies (as examples, the need to monitor presenter talk time as compared with participant talk time and the importance of utilizing a variety of practice-based teaching methods such as simulations, case studies, etc.)

Ultimately, as a result of the collaboration during the symposium, a sense of collective responsibility and shared accountability for program results, that had not existed previously, was created among the faculty. Already, KIPP is seeing an increase in faculty connections and the use of shared language across courses.

Furthermore, for KIPP, the curriculum is more than just an accumulation of sessions. How it is delivered is just as important as what is delivered. Both program staff and faculty are intentional about modeling behaviors and common language at all times. Rituals and routines help fellows make connections between what is being taught and their applications in schools. For example, at the opening of each Summer Institute course, KIPP has established a routine of stating the Competency Framework criteria being addressed in the session before introducing the faculty member. By articulating the learning standard upfront, staff members help fellows make connections and keep in mind the big-picture framework, and, ultimately, are modeling for fellows the importance of rituals and routines in their own communication with their teachers and staff once they are school leaders.

Residency/Experiential In-School Practice

The residency, or in-school experiential component, helps the fellow take what he or she has learned through coursework and apply it in practice. (The majority of the RLA programs have a program-arranged residency with a mentor-principal, though a few higher-education RLA members instead simply require a separate, unconnected teaching or administrative position in an urban school with leadership opportunities.) All of the programs ensure that

In reading this chapter, you may want to consider these Key Questions as you plan your training and development strategy.

> What are the objectives of the residency, and are they effectively captured in the ILP? Is the site likely to allow these objectives to be met?

> How will the residency experience link with the coursework and ongoing feedback/coaching?

> How long will the residency last? How long is necessary to acquire the critical learning and get adequate leadership practice? How quickly will a fellow be expected to move into a principalship? Will the residency be in one school or multiple schools and what are the benefits of both options? Will the fellow see an exemplar school? Will residency schools be similar to the kinds of schools the fellow is likely to be placed in as a principal?

> How are mentor-principals selected, trained, and matched with fellows? How is the school site selected? How will the mentor-principal, coach, and fellow all communicate and coordinate around goals and progress?

> Is funding available to pay a fellow's salary during a full-time residency period? Or will fellows complete training in addition to their current position—or somehow while in their current position? Can the assistant principal (AP) position be repurposed?

> What assessments will be used to evaluate the fellow during the in-school practice component? Are there concrete, articulated measures of success/completion?

their fellows have an opportunity to lead and manage adults, give feedback, and evaluate their work. RLA members believe strongly that fellows learn the most from actually engaging in the work, making mistakes, and building on successes. Ongoing feedback from a mentor-principal, a coach, a cohort peer, and/or others accelerates this learning and is something RLA programs universally value.

RLA programs are careful to tie the residency experiences to the ILPs of the fellows. For example, at the **University of Illinois at Chicago**, the residency begins after one-and-a-half semesters of coursework so the program already has significant information to shape an ILP. Before the school-based experience starts, the fellow, the mentor-principal, and the coach spend the month of July together reviewing the ILP and designing learning goals and strategies for the residency year.

RLA programs take different approaches to the residency, but all require a hands-on opportunity to take on real leadership, expect fellows to make a positive impact, and have mentor-principals. The following illustrate the variation in residency design:

Gwinnett County Public Schools: Two 25-day residencies at different schools.[10] Fellows maintain their roles as assistant principals during the training year, with substitutes covering their regular jobs during their residency experiences. Fellows also gain leadership experience while in their current positions, which is a less-expensive approach than a full-year residency.

KIPP Fisher Fellows: Approximately 10 weeks rotating among several schools (both KIPP schools and outstanding schools outside its charter network). While there is variability in how these experiences are structured, a fellow typically has sustained periods in two schools, some exposure to a new KIPP school, and a mix of school visits to gather effective practices. KIPP matches fellows to particular schools and leaders with strengths that align with the developmental goals of the individual. The program also believes it is important to spend time in a model school(s) and see what excellence looks like in real practice.

New Leaders for New Schools, NYC Leadership Academy, and the **University of Illinois at Chicago:** A full-year residency at one school plus visits to other schools (and for Leadership Academy, an additional six-week opportunity at a different school site). The residency period gives fellows the chance to see a full year of school operations and play a significant role in running a school. Fellows see the consequences of their actions, and learn to live with their mistakes.

RLA programs with similar goals may choose to structure their residencies differently, as demonstrated in the following example.

EXAMPLE

The **KIPP School Leadership Program** customizes its residency experiences by giving the fellow the opportunity to rotate through schools to accommodate each individual's leadership development goals. (See Appendix E for more information on the KIPP Residency.) Fellows who are new to leading teams may spend a concentrated amount of time in one school to immerse themselves in the culture and gain experience building teams. KIPP fellows who need practice using data might benefit from being in a few schools to learn from leaders and to see a variety of practices in action, and then moving to a new school where they could apply their learning firsthand.

In general, during the residency period, KIPP fellows are expected to:
- Gain behind-the-scenes insight into the instructional, operational, and people management practices of successful school leaders
- Gather and synthesize ideas from high-performing schools to inform their own School Design Plans
- Reflect upon and implement their learning from Summer Institute and Intersessions in a school setting
- Contribute to the host school utilizing the leadership competencies outlined as strengths on their ILPs
- Take on roles and/or manage projects that allow them to practice the areas of development on their Individualized Leadership Plans
- Perform tasks and actively participate in the day-to-day instructional, operational, or people management of the host school

This rotational approach contrasts with the **NYC Leadership Academy**, which assigns each aspiring principal to a 10-month residency in a school, with a six-week switch residency at another school so they can experience a different leadership style. By being in one location for the majority of the year, the participant gets to experience the opening of a new school year at a school and observe the types of experiences and changes that occur and take effect over the course of that year. This residency structure also enables participants to make decisions and then deal with the consequences of those decisions. The residency length allows them to take on real leadership opportunities at the school, including leading groups of adults. During the switch residency, they may be strategically placed in a school that has a particular program (i.e., bilingual) that matches their likely placement after graduation. While that is not always possible, the placement is aligned to introduce the candidate to a population or unique instructional approach that is different from what their primary residency offers. What is important to the Leadership Academy is having the candidate understand the entry process into a new school and how to quickly immerse into a different culture. By having this second entry experience, participants are able to apply their learning from the primary residency to this more short-term experience. This helps prepare them for entry into their job placement upon graduation.

No matter the structure, RLA members strive to make the residency as realistic and authentic as possible. Shadowing a principal is not enough. The fellows need to have the opportunity to engage in the work. Ideally, residents spend time leading significant projects within the school, giving them firsthand experience in practicing and developing necessary skills for the principalship. Examples of residency experiences and projects include:

> *RLA members believe strongly that fellows learn the most from actually engaging in the work, making mistakes, and building on successes. Ongoing feedback from a mentor-principal, a coach, a cohort peer, and/or others accelerates this learning and is something RLA programs universally value.*

- Participating in authentic leadership experiences, including debriefing major leadership decisions/actions with the principal on a regular basis
- Implementing a new math curriculum in two grade levels
- Developing and implementing a plan for improving student achievement using assessment data across multiple grades
- Having supervisory responsibility (and accountability) for a small number of teachers, including many opportunities for observations and feedback
- Developing and implementing an innovative program and measuring its effectiveness

While the residency/ experiential learning component is a learning opportunity for the fellow, it is also a time to deliver results for a school and its students, or at least a subset of students. RLA programs have generally pushed to have residents take responsibility for significant work such as supervising teachers or a grade-level team to have real accountability, tracking their results and showing improvement. **New Leaders for New Schools**, for example, is very clear in setting the expectation upfront with residents, mentor-principals, and coaches that residents will be held responsible for growth in specific classrooms, one grade, or one subject area. They are accountable for improving teacher practice and moving student achievement results approximately 10 percentage points within the year, generally measured though interim assessments.

The Importance of Mentor-Principal and School Site Selection

The school site for the residency and the mentor-principal are carefully (as carefully as context and the partnership with any district/CMO allow) targeted to the fellow's learning needs. RLA programs believe both are significant factors in a resident's learning, but given the choice, the right mentor-principal is of greater importance. (Unfortunately, not all programs with district partners feel they have adequate say over the choice of the mentor-principal and school site, which can be a significant constraint.)

For RLA members, it is unrealistic to expect to find mentors who are close to "perfect principals" and model effective practices in every area, but they must have expertise and skill in areas where the fellow needs to grow and be reflective about their practice. RLA programs aim to have mentor-principals who:

- Demonstrate high capacity to help train the fellow in his/her specific growth areas
- Can give the fellow space/opportunity to practice and make mistakes, including delegating high-stakes, authentic projects to the fellow
- Are invested in the fellow's progress and willing to guide his/her development
- Have leadership skills that align with program goals
- Demonstrate openness to sharing their reasoning for decision-making, including a willingness to share mistakes
- Are able to commit the time needed for regular debriefing and planning sessions

The mentor relationship is an essential component of the principal development period and many RLA programs conduct rigorous recruitment and selection processes for mentor-principals. Some more mature programs attempt to use mainly graduates of their own programs as mentor-principals, which ensures some consistency and increases the likelihood of commitment to the resident. In some cases, the district compensates the mentor-principal for the extra responsibility to ensure that they feel responsible for their role. Other programs opt not to pay to avoid setting up a financial incentive to do the work or additional political issues around who is selected, and have found people willing to volunteer.

In the past, **KIPP School Leadership Program** Residency Hosts have self-selected and volunteered to be mentor-principals. KIPP has also started using Healthy Schools data to help place fellows to make sure they are working with effective mentor-principals. Healthy Schools data measure key elements of school health across the network, including on-the-ground practices and conditions that make a school healthy and are leading indicators for improved student achievement outcomes. (More information on the Healthy Schools initiative can be found on page 111 of the *Supporting Principals* chapter.)

SEE PAGE 111

Learn more in the Supporting Principals chapter.

Important to RLA programs—although usually secondary to mentor-principal match—is selecting a school site that is a good match to the school the resident expects or hopes to lead as a principal. School settings and needs vary widely depending on grade-level configuration, whether it is an established school or a start-up, functionality of the school, and accountability designation (turnaround or transformation, for instance).

Coaching/Providing Ongoing Feedback

The RLA programs agree that it is critically important to support and give regular, ongoing feedback to the fellows throughout the training and development phase as the fellow's learning curve needs to remain steep the entire year. As fellows consolidate learning through action at the residency school site and extend themselves as leaders using practices and ideas they have just learned, they need a reflective mirror. One key attribute most programs look for in the selection process is openness to feedback and willingness to continually learn—because most RLA programs believe that it is feedback (often provided by a coach) coupled with practice that accelerates learning.

> RLA programs stress the importance of having a coherent and cohesive curriculum that effectively organizes and integrates central ideas so fellows can see how the ideas build on or connect with other ideas, enabling them to develop new understandings and skills.

In addition to the mentor-principal, RLA programs often draw on the expertise of former practitioners and leadership experts (coaches) to help facilitate learning, provide constructive criticism, and offer ongoing support throughout the training and development phase. This can take the form of coaching, but RLA programs agree it is not necessarily the specific structure of having a coach that matters. What does matter is that fellows have the opportunity to:

▶ Interact on a regular basis with an outside informed observer who has significant experience in school leadership
▶ Receive ongoing feedback to accelerate development and growth
▶ Reflect on lessons learned and self-evaluate
▶ Be asked questions to help them process their experience
▶ Be supported as they work through problems and define action steps

In fact, RLA programs think about coaching as an action or a strategy rather than a particular person's role. Coaching can be done by many different people: mentor, facilitator, faculty, or a peer. It is not about the title of coach but ensuring that fellows are given ongoing, constructive, and critical feedback. While most RLA programs do choose to assign coaches, they have experimented with different models over the past several years trying to find the right balance so that coaching is effective, consistent, guided by the learning goals of the fellow, and based in the experience of the residency and yet not reactive. Each has developed a slightly different approach based on program context, resources, and lessons learned over time.

The **KIPP School Leadership Program**, for example, has strengthened its model of using Leadership Guides as coaches during Summer Institute to help participants link course learning to their specific, individual development goals and to their experiences in their own school environments. Previously, the program had assigned program staff to coach fellows during the Institute. This was not a very effective model as the staff had other responsibilities and not all the staff had experience as principals. Now, KIPP identifies successful, practicing principals within the KIPP network and prepares them to be Leadership Guides during the summer. KIPP believes this model is much more robust, a sentiment reflected by participants who consistently report that the Leadership Guides are a critical component of the Summer Institute experience.

For most RLA programs, the coach is usually on staff, as compared to a mentor-principal employed by the district or CMO hosting the residency. For some, the coach serves as a classic executive coach and supports the development of personal leadership skills. For others, the coach serves as a comprehensive principal coach and helps fellows learn all skills and experiences necessary for principalship, focusing on school improvement. In some cases, the coach isn't one individual, but a combination of people with different perspectives and expertise to draw from and align to fellows' needs.

Aligning coaching to the ILP and the Competency Framework is key so that the coach avoids being reactive (commiserating, sharing stories, or getting pulled into the crisis of the moment). Instead the coach is guided by the development plan and keeps the fellow focused on it. **New Leaders for New Schools**, for instance, expects coaches to collect specific evidence tied to the ILP's five priority areas: 1) learning and teaching; 2) school culture; 3) aligning staff; 4) systems and operations; and 5) personal leadership. New Leaders for New Schools believes this systematic and deliberate approach to coaching (setting a standard, making an individual development plan, and documenting evidence of success and growth) results in improved resident capacity and greater student achievement.

RLA programs find that the more targeted the ILP, the more a coach—or other person providing feedback—can focus on observing specific growth areas in action (e.g., running professional development, observing teachers, having difficult conversations), and providing effective feedback. The coach can also see fellows' progression and understand where they are developing proficient skills and where they need more opportunities to develop. The observational evidence coaches collect and track guides the development process.

K?

In reading this chapter, you may want to consider these Key Questions as you plan your training and development strategy.

> What guidance, support, and feedback are necessary to effectively develop an aspiring principal?

> If coaches are to be used, how will they be selected, trained, and evaluated?

> What will be the length of the coaching period, taking into account the speed of entry into the principalship and the type of school the fellow is likely to lead?

> What specific areas will the coach be responsible for helping the fellow develop?

> What are the goals of coaching? Is it a focus on personal leadership? Is the emphasis more on school improvement? Or is it some combination of the two?

> Will the coach assigned to the fellow be an outside confidant? Will the coach play a role in evaluating or supervising, or only in developing the fellow?

DEPLOYMENT OF COACHES

Coaches working with fellows during training may continue on through at least the first year of the fellow's tenure as a principal, depending on the program model. Some programs believe coaches should be expert either in fellow training and development, or in support of principals and should be different people; others believe consistency of relationship is paramount and thus have the resident coach follow the principal into his/her first year on the job. Residency coaching, discussed in this section, focuses on the fellow's development in preparation for assuming the principal role. Principal coaching, discussed in the *Supporting Principals* chapter of this document, emphasizes driving whole-school achievement forward, ongoing growth, and the on-the-job issues encountered once the fellow has actually assumed the principal role.

Finding and Preparing Strong Coaches

It is difficult to find people with the right level of experience and characteristics to be effective coaches. RLA programs look for experienced, effective school leaders who have the beliefs, content expertise, interpersonal skills, and, often, coaching ability. RLA programs are more and more deliberate about the skill sets coaches must have, although some training is also usually provided to facilitate coaches' growth.

Most RLA programs look for people who are highly effective at improving schools and implementing effective practices. Because coaching is labor- and time-intensive, it is not the right job for many retired principals. They have to be passionate about improving student outcomes and willing to work long hours to support the next generation of school leaders. These capable coaches are used to doing the work themselves and may not have the skills to facilitate and support others on the job. Therefore, RLA programs invest in training their coaches on how to be good listeners, facilitators, and collaborators. They also need to stay current on the latest research, issues affecting educational leadership, and effective school practices. (See *Appendix E* for more detailed RLA program explanations on identifying and choosing coaches.)

Learn more in Appendix E.

SEE PAGE 172

NYC Leadership Academy faculty members embody multiple roles of classroom instructor and coach. These "facilitators" design and implement the curriculum over the summer and one-and-a-half days a week during the year; they also are expected to do residency school visits and support the work of participants in the school. The benefit of this model is that there is a consistent person who is monitoring growth in the classroom and at the school site.

Finding staff with the pedagogical background and success leading a school, strong content expertise, and a facilitative stance is challenging. The facilitator must be very skilled in modeling the kinds of behavior the program expects participants and the mentor-principals in the residency sites to exhibit. Usually the Leadership Academy taps former practitioners—superintendents and/or principals—who have solid school leadership experience, but who may not have well-developed facilitation skills. The Leadership Academy finds that it is easier to train former practitioners to become effective facilitators than to train effective facilitators to become skilled in leadership development or school improvement strategies.

The Leadership Academy trains program faculty to help participants make meaning of the work through facilitation that is inquiry-based and aimed at building participants' leadership capacities. As facilitators, they seek to nurture the three-way partnership between participants, mentor-principals, and program staff, which provides a rich feedback loop that benefits the participant and the mentor-principal in powerful ways.

Approaches to Coaching

RLA programs have varying approaches to coaching and even in how they define the term.

The **University of Illinois at Chicago** is committed to coaching; their faculty see no better way to help aspiring principals stay on a fast-paced developmental trajectory and be ready to lead transformational change in Chicago schools. UIC coaches come together at the beginning of each semester to review the course syllabi and make connections between classroom and school-based experiences, taking into account individual growth needs. The coaches visit fellows at their schools at least weekly to help track progress toward their learning goals, participate in classroom visits, attend teacher meetings, and then debrief with the fellow to process what has been learned. The coaches use a Socratic method of questioning designed to push the fellow to reflect on his/her performance, digest the experience, and take meaning from it.

For **KIPP** Fisher Fellows, leadership coaching is multi-faceted. All coaching is built around an individualized development plan. During the Summer Institute, fellows are paired with a Leadership Guide (as on page 83). Throughout the remainder of the programming year, they are paired with both an executive leadership coach and another staff member (former high-performing principal). The conversations between the executive leadership coach and the fellow are confidential and not shared with the rest of the program staff nor used for evaluative purposes—a distinguishing feature of the KIPP model. In contrast, the conversations between the program staff coach and the fellow are not confidential and center on progress toward identified goals and milestones in the individualized development plan, and are used in the evaluation process to determine readiness for the principalship. Coaches and fellows meet biweekly for approximately an hour.

New Leaders for New Schools coaches visit schools at least biweekly to observe meetings, conduct professional development, and participate in classroom walkthroughs, teacher observations, and conferences with the fellow. The coach and fellow then debrief what they saw and talk about the implications. This evidence-based approach to coaching goes deeper than a theoretical conversation about leadership challenges, which makes the coaching relationship powerful. The coach is responsible for ensuring that the fellow plays a significant role in driving student achievement gains (for at least a subset of the student population), ultimately making the coach and fellow responsible for results.

In some cases, programs forgo coaches and use peer feedback and support instead. **REEP**, for example, has chosen a peer-coaching model. The program found it difficult to identify high-quality mentors who could coach transformative leaders. Therefore, REEP looks for facilitative skills as part of its selection process to ensure that fellows have the capacity to support and coach others while in the program. Trust and cohort unity are very important to establish upfront, as is the need to minimize personal and professional conflicts. During group forums, peer mentors share and discuss challenges and problem-solve together. REEP staff members also meet with fellows on an individual basis to attend to any specific leadership issues or needs.

Most RLA programs provide coach training to ensure that coaches have an in-depth understanding of the program mission and goals, stay abreast of the most effective coach and school practices and district context, and to ensure consistency in the coaching model.

The level of coach preparation varies within RLA programs. For the **University of Illinois at Chicago**, Chicago Public Schools provides the most formal training through its Blended Coaching[11] training sessions. In addition, UIC has a coach supervisor who leads the coaches in weekly meetings (the weeks alternate: one week they meet as a group, the next week each coach meets individually with the coach supervisor). These regular conversations ensure that the coaches stay on track and give fellows the support and modeling they need. The meetings also serve as a training tool for the coaches as the supervisor provides guidance and can send in extra supports or resources if a resident or school is struggling.

RLA programs also devise tools and techniques to help their coaches be effective. **NYC Leadership Academy**, for example, is exploring the use of video in capturing effective coaching conversations. By creating a mini-library of videos, the program may be able to use the virtual sessions as training tools to help build the coaching skills of its facilitators. Videos can demonstrate important aspects of coaching such as how to get the conversation started, build trust, give feedback, and stay neutral. **New Leaders for New Schools'** Effective Practices Incentive Community (EPIC) program has created an online library of effective leadership practices and resources, including videos and lesson plans. EPIC is aligned to New Leaders for New Schools' coaching framework and its content materials are used in coach trainings as well as resident coursework.

Cohort Support/Culture of Continuous Improvement

RLA members have noted the power of having a strong cohort of peers who push each other to improve and grow. Though these peers do not have dedicated time to "coach," often they are able to provide powerful, honest feedback to each other. Those who are selected to join the program typically share similar high expectations, a sense of urgency and eagerness to affect change, and a drive to improve student outcomes. As they progress through the program together, they are likely to form strong bonds and mutual trust through shared experiences. By having a community of practice where they can share insights and exchange feedback, fellows advance their learning. The **KIPP School Leadership Program**, for example, has a strong culture of community, trust, and openness. The Summer Institute incorporates time for learning teams of four to five fellows to meet twice a week. Each person is expected to plan and facilitate two meetings during the Summer Institute, with peers giving feedback on the performance. This not only gives school leaders practice setting agendas, planning meetings, facilitating group dynamics, and pushing for outcomes, but it also builds a strong peer network and the routine of peers giving specific, meaningful feedback, both positive and critical. This culture of professionalism where anyone is free to provide advice and suggestions pervades the KIPP model and serves its fellows well.

Evaluation and Assessment of the Fellow

RLA members have taken the necessary steps to invest in the development of systems that support ongoing evaluation and continuous improvement. This is an extremely complex undertaking that involves staff at all levels (faculty, coach, mentor) providing extensive and ongoing feedback.

Throughout the program, feedback about a fellow's progress and ultimate progression to the principalship is transparent and linked to the Competency Framework and the ILP. RLA programs are designed to give fellows regular and candid feedback and to assess at the end of the program whether a fellow is ready to be a principal, an assistant principal, or neither. Periodic benchmark assessments are built into the development process, usually at the beginning of the program (coming primarily from self-assessment and selection process data), formative assessments throughout the training, and a summative assessment at the end of the program. All of the RLA programs have some significant self-assessment against their own competencies as a critical part of the evaluation process—first to target growth areas and then to capture a fellow's own experience of his/her growth. Ultimately, fellows need to demonstrate proficiency in all of the Competency Framework areas in order to enter the principalship (with the recognition that they will continue to develop their skills on the job).

Most RLA programs provide coach training to ensure that coaches have an in-depth understanding of the program mission and goals, and stay abreast of the most effective coaching practices.

Did the individual meet the standards outlined in the Competency Framework?

What progress did the fellow make on his/her targeted growth areas (i.e. are they proficient on all the Competency Framework areas)?

Were the fellows hired as principals or assistant principals after completing the program?

If they were hired, what was their retention and success level on the job, especially in moving student achievement?

In reading this chapter, you may want to consider these Key Questions as you plan your training and development strategy.

Dismissal Needs to Be an Option

The residency year/development period is a critical time when a program can understand if a fellow is ready to become a principal. RLA programs are careful to use the regular feedback cycles to give the fellows multiple opportunities to improve. Most program models rely on the participant's willingness and ability to work furiously and develop quickly. For a variety of reasons this does not always happen as predicted. In rare cases, if the fellow fails to meet necessary benchmarks, RLA programs staff determine whether the fellow should be dismissed, or whether an alternative placement, such as an assistant principalship, is necessary to adequately prepare him or her to be a principal.

While RLA programs are committed to the development of their fellows, they all see their primary client as students. RLA programs say it is more beneficial to de-select someone in the development process than allow a weak person to continue, as a poor-performing principal may have a significantly negative impact on students. RLA programs have de-selection rates between 2 and 20 percent each year.

COST AND RESOURCE ALLOCATION CONSIDERATIONS

It is important to keep in mind that training and development are likely to be the most expensive aspects of the principal preparation program. RLA members make choices about how to structure their programs that take into account available funds and resources. The residency component is the most expensive as the fellow often gets paid a salary during the school-based experience (sometimes an AP salary, sometimes a teacher salary). Coaching is also an expensive component, involving significant paid staff time. Cost factors to consider when designing a training and development model include:

▷ Number of fellows (including considerations of economies of scale to be gained)
▷ Length of coursework and frequency of in-person time and travel, if necessary
▷ Length of residency and resident salary
▷ Length of coaching experience and fellow-to-coach ratio

Evaluation and Assessment of the Training Program

RLA members evaluate their faculty and coaches on a regular basis to ensure that the fellows are getting top-notch instruction, training, support, and guidance. For example, **KIPP** has a long-established method for giving faculty immediate feedback on their delivery. Participants submit online surveys on a daily basis rating the rigor and relevance of the content and instructor effectiveness. KIPP shares this information with the faculty, allowing for continued implementation of what is working effectively and for adjustment of what is not working. If the feedback overwhelmingly suggests room for improvement in areas such as instructional pacing, engagement, or rigor, the faculty members are expected to adjust their teaching methods accordingly. KIPP uses these data to set high expectations of quality and ensure that the courses offer valuable, practical information. KIPP does not hesitate to remove faculty who are not up to standard even in real-time of a multi-day module.

The ability to be flexible and make mid-course corrections if needed is key to RLA programs' success. Frequent evaluations (including course evaluations, surveys of fellows and staff, focus groups, etc.) allow RLA programs to assess the impact of their curriculum and its delivery.

RLA members also use data collected throughout the recruitment, selection, and training and development processes to provide more cumulative and long-term evaluations and assessments relating to their own programs and the field at large. These data feed a constant loop of continuous improvement. For example, programs fine-tune their training and development experiences based on strengths and weaknesses in the performance of their principals and their schools in years one through five.

In reading this chapter, you may want to consider these Key Questions as you plan your training and development strategy.

> What do participant satisfaction surveys tell us upon graduation? One year out? Two years out?

> How did fellows progress on the Competency Framework throughout training and at the end of the program compared with the beginning, before training?

> What percentage of the fellows completed the program successfully by meeting the Competency Framework expectations? Were they placed in schools with a good fit?

> What was the feedback from coaches and support staff?

Lessons Learned

Based on their years of practice and experience, RLA programs highlight the following overarching lessons when thinking through the training and development process:

1 *The training and development process may vary but the focus on outcomes does not.* While each of the RLA programs approach coursework, residency, and coaching differently, they all develop ILPs that map out in great detail the training and development sequence needed to secure effective principal competencies and result in improved student outcomes.

2 *Focus on developing what was not selected for.* As discussed in the *Selecting Candidates* chapter, candidates are selected with some traits and skills intact and others needing further development. Training is used to fill any remaining gaps after assessing the skills of the selected cohort and reinforce what is already intact. The more areas that need to be trained, the more intensive and costly the program will be.

3 *Consider the district environment and schools' operating context.* Context influences every decision in the design of training and development. Some variables to consider are the coordination and cohesiveness of district/CMO operations and management; depth of experience with candidates before they enter the program; and school placement. Some RLA programs are being more proactive and engaging and partnering with districts when designing their development sequences.

4 *Fellows need to engage in authentic leadership experiences that involve real leadership of adults on behalf of students.* Shadowing and observing other leaders is not sufficient preparation. Fellows need to play a significant role, make decisions, and learn from their mistakes.

5 *Delivery of coursework is about modeling leadership and affording opportunities for fellows to practice.* RLA programs are very cognizant of the fact that what they model in their professional development delivery and leadership training impacts fellows as much as the content itself. Fellows benefit from multiple opportunities to practice, debrief about decision points, get feedback, and try again, building their confidence and skills. Fellows also learn from role-plays and observations of program staff in real-time in all that they do as they manage the program and internalize cues about leadership. Taking time to make these leadership lessons explicit is important.

6 *Coaching is one method of providing ongoing feedback, but not the only way.* While most RLA programs have invested in some form of coaching role to provide regular feedback and support to the fellow, the more important point is establishing a powerful network of experts, practitioners, and peers who can give feedback regularly during the training year.

A Look Ahead: Supporting Principals

RLA programs do not end their relationship with their graduating fellow at the point of program completion. These programs offer a series of supports to help their graduates to transition into new schools and to quickly strengthen the instructional experience and academic outcomes of students. Various RLA approaches are summarized in the next chapter, *Supporting Principals.*

Supporting
Principals

5

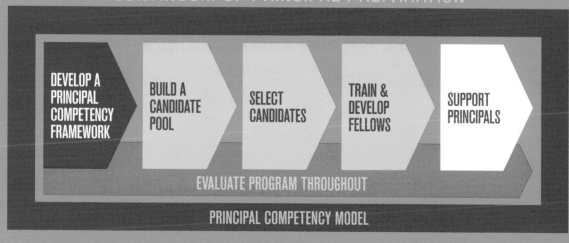

CONTINUUM OF PRINCIPAL PREPARATION

DEVELOP A PRINCIPAL COMPETENCY FRAMEWORK

BUILD A CANDIDATE POOL

SELECT CANDIDATES

TRAIN & DEVELOP FELLOWS

SUPPORT PRINCIPALS

EVALUATE PROGRAM THROUGHOUT

PRINCIPAL COMPETENCY MODEL

5

SUPPORTING PRINCIPALS | Because RLA programs are committed to improving student achievement, their relationship with their fellows does not end at graduation. These programs support their new graduates by *helping them identify and secure job placements* in schools with needs that best match up with their strengths. They also provide *ongoing support to graduates* in the form of professional development and ongoing coaching to help them grow on the job. While RLA programs want their graduates to be successful as individuals, they have a greater interest in mind: driving change in the school as a whole. Therefore, some RLA programs provide not only individual support, but whole-school support in the form of leadership team trainings and school-wide evaluations of effectiveness. In addition, some RLA programs have begun to engage at the district and state levels to influence policies and practices that can either help or hinder principals in their efforts to build and sustain successful schools.

Support of Principals

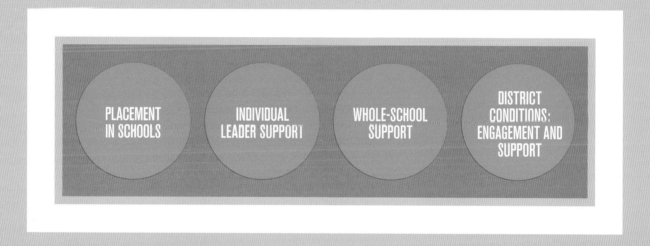

The intensity and complexity of the principalship cannot be overstated, especially in underserved schools. Balancing all of the components of the principalship is often challenging for a new principal. First-year principals endeavor to build a strong school culture, establish a collaborative professional community, and understand and use data with teachers to drive improvements in student outcomes. They may struggle to integrate their personal sense of urgency for improved student achievement with their ability to lead and engage adults in the change process. Through support of new principals, RLA programs aim to ensure that their principals have an immediate impact on school culture and climate and in leading efforts to improve the quality of instruction and long-term student achievement.

In addition to helping principals be effective, principal support helps with retention on the job, and by extension, improved student achievement. The principalship can be a lonely job; support helps mediate against the isolation and retain effective leaders. Principals are critical to the school improvement process and a study by Fuller and Young shows they must stay there a number of consecutive years to fully affect a school.[12] The same study shows that principal and teacher retention are linked: Schools with high levels of principal retention typically have higher levels of retention of quality teachers. Keeping high-quality principals in place, therefore, helps to keep strong teachers in a school.

Most RLA programs use support for the *individual leader* as the primary lever for school change, first helping graduates find principalships and then supporting them within these positions. Some also choose to provide supplemental support at the whole-school or broader school leadership team level. A few are engaging at the district level to help ensure that district conditions and policies are proactively working to support principals trying to transform schools and drive student achievement gains.

Each of the levels of principal support highlighted in the graphic above is discussed in some detail in the remainder of this chapter. RLA programs take different approaches to balance these types of support.

While RLA programs want their graduates to be successful as individuals, they have a greater interest in mind: driving change in the school as a whole.

Placement

The first step in helping fellows secure job placement is assessing their strengths and skills before the hiring process begins. With this information, programs identify openings and work with the district/CMO to the extent possible to understand school circumstances and determine best fit. Once graduates are in the applicant pool for particular jobs, programs help them prepare for interviews by researching the local context and school data, briefing them on the interview process, and helping them practice for the various interview steps.

What are the placement opportunities in the district or CMOs and what is the process to match the graduates with the right-fit opportunities?

How will you work with your partner districts and CMOs throughout your program year to understand their needs and shape their understanding of your candidates?

What support will your first-year principals need and what role will you play in providing it? Will you differentiate levels of support?

Will you offer any services to leaders beyond their first year? If so, what? Will you differentiate these?

Will your support focus mainly on the leader (like executive coaching), the school as a whole, or some combination of the two?

If you are not the district or CMO but an external partner, will you try to influence district practices, structures, and systems to support principals? Will you try to get alignment with the district or CMO by influencing their practices or changing yours?

G?

In reading this chapter, you may want to reflect back on these Guiding Questions as you plan support options within your program.

How will you assess the strengths and talents of your program's graduates? How will this information be shared with potential schools and districts?

How many positions are open? What grade level? What is the circumstance of each school?

Who is the hiring manager within the district/CMO and how can you get him/her to know fellows and program alumni well?

What percentage of your graduates do you expect to be placed as principals upon graduation? Within one year? What level of accountability does your program take to make this happen? Is placement as an Assistant Principal an acceptable outcome? Under what circumstances?

Assessing the Strengths and Skills of Graduates

Through the recruitment, selection, and training and development phases, RLA programs come to know their fellows well. While graduates need to be proficient in all program competency areas, there will be some areas in which they are particularly adept. By identifying their strengths, programs can be more explicit in their placement recommendations. For instance, some graduates may be very good at change management, interpersonal relations, and systems reform to help bring resistant staff on board and improve failing systems. These candidates may be best suited for turnaround schools with inherited, returning staff and broken systems. Others will be better at building new systems, creating partnerships, and being more entrepreneurial. These candidates are ideal for start-up school arrangements where structures have to be initiated and staff hired.

Upon program completion, most RLA programs conduct a "readiness inventory" of each of the graduates against the Competency Framework, in order to assess their skills, knowledge, and dispositions, as well as judge whether they are ready for the principalship. This summative assessment is used to determine optimal school placement. Program completers also self-assess using the readiness inventory and articulate any preferences regarding location, school type, size, and culture. RLA programs seek to have a transparent assessment process throughout the year. They want no surprising information for fellows.

There is a very open and honest conversation among program staff and graduates about areas of strength and weakness and how to identify and attain the best placement match. In limited cases, when the graduate is not ready for the principalship, RLA programs may suggest an assistant principal position. It is important that these assistant principal positions are carefully selected and can afford the graduate significant instructional leadership responsibilities to foster further development.

Understanding School Needs

In addition to summarizing the strengths and capabilities of program completers, programs also need to work with target districts/CMOs to assess the characteristics and needs of schools with vacant positions. To do this, programs need strong, open, communicative relationships with someone in their partner school organizations. What are the demands of each job? What is the school context? How will each school benefit from a slightly different leadership profile? Here are some examples:

▸ **A school in restructuring** likely has a history of ineffective adult practices, such as weak teaching, and declining student performance. For this school, the most important leader strengths are being able to overcome the inertia of previous failures; promote the belief that all students can achieve at high levels; manage teachers effectively by helping them improve their practices; and support a change management process. If the leader is expected to replace significant portions of staff, strong interviewing and hiring skills are also critical.

▸ **A start-up school** will be built from the ground up. For this school, it is critical that a principal have a vision for the school and be able to articulate it. The start-up principal must be a strong entrepreneur who is able to overcome obstacles and have strong project management skills to manage all of the details ranging from establishing the school's academics and hiring staff to recruiting students, planning the physical space, and ordering furniture. This principal must be the master of multiple tasks.

▸ **A "status quo" school** may be performing well but could be challenged to move from "good to great." In this circumstance, a principal may encounter resistance from existing staff who are satisfied with current systems and methods. This principal must instill a sense of urgency; be able to use data to continually examine and diagnose what is working and what is not working well; and be able to coach staff in more effective practices.

PLACEMENT OPPORTUNITIES ARE CONSIDERED EARLY

Placement is considered early on throughout the development period as well. As mentioned in the *Training and Developing Fellows* chapter, whenever possible, fellows are placed in residencies that are similar to their likely placement upon program completion. There they focus on developing strength in the particular areas they will likely need to be successful in that kind of setting. For example, if the fellow will most likely launch a new, small high school it is invaluable to participate in a start-up during the training year. Likewise, if a fellow is most likely to enter a turnaround-school context, working during the training year with a strong principal who is in the first year or two of a turnaround is immensely beneficial to the fellow's growth and understanding of the practices required in this setting.

Working with Districts and CMOs

Because RLA programs have a deep understanding of their alums' previous work histories, skill sets, knowledge, and dispositions they can help identify the particular school opportunities that best suit each individual and advise hiring managers on good-fit placements.

Typically, RLA programs designate a staff member who is responsible for developing a strong, amicable relationship with the partner district or CMO to ensure, as much as possible, that program completers are optimally placed, including learning of opportunities and communicating regularly with the contact. The earlier the process of getting to know fellows starts, the better. RLA programs share information about their graduates with the district contact, including assessments of their readiness against the Competency Framework, their strengths and areas of growth, as well as bios, résumés and references. Programs make determinations about what is appropriate to share (some data are confidential by law) and are very upfront with their graduates about the kinds of information that interested districts/CMOs will be given.

For example, the **New Leaders for New Schools** program in Washington, D.C., begins introducing the district hiring manager to its principal candidates while the candidates are in their residencies so they can form relationships and consider potential school matches. District and CMO staff may even participate in the selection process, and often attend workshops, join in the summer intensive training, and serve as guest facilitators or visiting workshop leaders. The program also prepares a booklet with a picture and bio of each fellow, their key strengths, and their best types of placement match to give to districts and CMOs in anticipation of graduation from the program. Program staff members arrange meetings with district hiring managers to review candidate profiles and discuss placement opportunities with human resources, assistant superintendents, and the Leadership Director.

RLA programs have found that the more honest and open a program can be about accurately assessing a particular candidate's skill sets, the more likely the district/CMO will come to rely on the program for placement recommendations. RLA programs are also careful to convey their viewpoints about what makes an effective school leader. Their graduates may not fit the more traditional principal profile and, especially for new programs that do not yet have a track record of success, districts/CMOs might need to be convinced to take a chance on their graduates. For instance, in one particular RLA partner district, the traditional principal was an African American male in his mid-50s who focused on operations. In contrast, the majority of this particular program's graduates are African American women in their mid-30s who excel in instructional leadership. Because this profile does not match with district or community panel hiring expectations, program graduates may be overlooked. The program takes an active leadership role to change the perception of what a principal "looks like" and help district leaders to be comfortable and confident in the skills, knowledge, and dispositions that RLA graduates bring to the job.

Some RLA programs have begun to engage at the district and state levels to influence policies and practices that can either help or hinder principals in their efforts to build and sustain successful schools.

The connection and depth of the relationship between a program and a target district/CMO varies widely. As mentioned throughout this document, the context of the program matters; circumstances dictate how involved the program can be in placing its graduates. Some programs are external to the district or CMOs, while other program operators are the district or CMO themselves. No matter their level of control in the hiring process, all RLA programs aim to graduate high-quality candidates who are likely to succeed in the principalship, as well as in the interview process to secure a principalship.

Preparing Fellows for Hire

In addition to making recommendations about the best matches for their graduates to school needs, RLA programs help their fellows prepare for the hiring process. To do so, programs learn the hiring process of the district/CMO and scrutinize school priorities and circumstances to help the candidate prepare. The deeper the relationship a program has with the district/CMO, the more nuance and detail it can provide to graduates. Some specific examples of assistance that RLA programs provide are:

- Résumé and cover letter models and writing support
- Timeline of hiring and key activities
- Mock interviews with debrief and feedback on performance
- Visits to schools expecting vacancies
- "Meet and greet" sessions with hiring managers
- Connections with sitting principals or teachers to get inside perspective

Once in the candidate pool and eligible for school-specific interviews, program graduates are expected to do their own homework on the district and school situation so that they are prepared to identify and discuss their responses to particular challenges. The school and district websites can be good sources of background information and context. Many programs expect their fellows to do an in-depth review of all available school data, both current and past years, so that they are familiar with trends, strengths, and areas that need attention. Finally, graduates are encouraged to visit the surrounding neighborhood to get a feel for the community.

After the school interview process, partner districts typically give RLA programs feedback about how their candidates did in each stage so they can continue to help their graduates present high-quality applications, as well as grow into stronger candidates. Districts may also debrief on their impressions of the cohort as a whole to help programs evaluate the effectiveness of their coursework, residency, and coaching components.

Support During the Principalship

The task of securing a position is only the first step. The job of principal is complex and the first year is especially challenging. Principals entering low-performing schools have an even more challenging start, as they have to act quickly on many fronts. They need to assess the current state of the school and identify the priority work in order to drive student achievement. Upon entry, they work quickly to influence the culture of the school, including establishing a core vision for the school and setting norms and expectations for behavior within the school. They also nurture leadership skills in other school employees, help teachers improve their instruction, and establish a sense of urgency for change. All the while, they attend to the myriad of other issues that arise as part of leading a community of students, teachers, and parents.

This is no small feat, even for the strongest leaders completing RLA programs. These programs provide support to their alumni on multiple fronts: *the individual leader*; at the *school level*; and at *the district or CMO level*, influencing and strengthening conditions and structures that can enable or detract from a principal's ability to perform his/her job. The majority of the RLA programs focus primarily on the individual leader and view school-level and district-level supports as supplemental. Each of these is discussed in turn on the following pages.

In reading this chapter, you may want to reflect back on these Key Questions as you plan support options within your program.

What kinds of support will be given to new hires as they enter their principalships?

Will services be differentiated based on individual leader needs, school needs (turnaround, start-up), and/or school grade level (elementary, middle, high)?

Will your program provide coaching? If so, how will you select and train coaches? Is their role to support the individual leader, the leadership team, the whole school, or some combination?

Is there a need for the program to weigh in on the district/CMO conditions needed to support new principals? If so, what policies and supports would be most beneficial?

How will your program evaluate the impact of support services?

Individual Leader Support

All RLA programs provide some direct support to their first-year principals—ranging from individual coaching by staff to peer coaching to ongoing workshops to access to experts. RLA programs stress the importance of driving continuous learning and development while also deeply supporting the focused school-improvement efforts needed to achieve academic gains. Through feedback (coaching) and professional development (targeted training), new principals are encouraged to deepen their skills and reflect on their own performance.

Coaching

Most RLA programs provide coaching to principals as they enter their new school. Coaches help principals to diagnose school needs and develop and monitor a responsive action plan. Support from experienced, effective educators can help new principals focus on the important things instead of the merely urgent. Coaching helps school leaders to do the kind of systemic and strategic thinking that creates real change. Coaching can be done one-on-one or as part of a cohort network of peers. RLA programs also continue to support those graduates who moved into assistant principalships and need additional coaching and time to develop. (See *Appendix F* for a description of the **Gwinnett County Public Schools** Quality-Plus Leader Academy mentor program for principals and assistant principals.)

> The intensity and complexity of the principalship cannot be overstated, especially in under-served schools.

SEE PAGE 194

Learn more
in Appendix F.

Coaches often help entering principals develop immediate school action plans (30 days, 60 days, 90 days) over the summer. They may accompany them to meetings at the school site before school starts to better understand the school context. The more that graduates can understand the school culture and climate, the more likely they will be to have a smooth entry and transition into their job. Individualized coaching may continue throughout the first year when principals have the steepest learning curve. Second-year and beyond supports vary by program as illustrated by these two examples:

NYC Leadership Academy provides coaching to first-year principals, which is paid for by the New York City Department of Education (Leadership Academy provides coaching for virtually all new New York City principals, Leadership Academy alums as well as others). Coaching is available for second-year principals (and beyond) who want to pay for it from their own budgets (principals often use Title II school funds to cover the expense).

New Leaders for New Schools concentrates on coaching its first-year principals, with a national policy of continued support into the second year only for principals of secondary schools, recognizing that high schools especially are more complex and challenging places to lead and manage. Leaders of schools that are struggling or more difficult to turn around may get extra support as needed at the regional level.

Post-program principal coaching is different from coaching during residency in that newly placed principals need more intense support on a wider range of issues. No longer are they "trying on the job" with a segment of teachers and students, they are the school leaders responsible for every aspect of school management and instructional leadership.

The **University of Illinois at Chicago** (UIC) provides coaches to help its new principals to develop concrete action plans for their schools based on the school improvement plan and a customized data system developed by UIC. The state and district summative data reports are repurposed to help principals and school leaders to dissect test results and drill down into the underlying complexities. All principals receive a data dashboard that norms the data (i.e., puts actual test scores on a normal distribution curve broken into quartiles comparing student performance statewide) so that principals can compare the state's four proficiency levels with four statewide quartiles. The dashboard also compares the percentage of students meeting/exceeding state standards with the percentage achieving at or above grade level. Then UIC presents the data in a more granular format (stanine distributions that scale test scores on a standard nine-point scale) that helps identify which students are, or are not, making progress on the achievement distribution. By presenting the data in a more meaningful and usable format, including school, grade, homeroom, and class roster files, the principal and teachers can target instruction at the classroom level. Because UIC has been creating these data dashboards for its graduates, and residents, for years, the system provides a longitudinal look at student progress year to year. This in-depth review helps principals to move beyond the post-mortem conversation about how they did on the state assessment to ask better questions and use the data in a more formative way.

In general, RLA programs are moving to more structured models of coaching that focus on critical leadership areas and proven practices that drive student achievement forward, rather than general leadership skill coaching. The **KIPP School Leadership Program** provides *both* confidential leadership coaching that focuses on the leader and his or her leadership skills and, through their regional leaders, structured content coaching on their school data indicators and performance goals when leaders are serving as principals.

Strong Coaching

New Leaders for New Schools has a coaching framework that clearly defines the role of the coach. Coaches are responsible for:

1) Using *analysis and action planning* to help the New Leader principal to focus on the right work for the school. This includes a diagnostic process implemented three times during the year that identifies which school practices need to be developed or improved in order to drive dramatic student achievement results. The diagnostic, coupled with a leadership assessment process, also implemented three times during the year, identifies which leadership skills the New Leader needs to further develop in order to drive change.

2) *Effectively using inquiry to drive deep thinking* of the New Leader principal, as well as the leadership team. Coaches are expected to question and lead principals to answers, without explicitly giving them the answers. The leadership team is an integrated, integral part of the work and the coach is responsible for building the skills of the principal to develop the capacity of the leadership team.

3) *Demonstrating knowledge of resources and practices* that drive large-scale improvements of the individual leader's practices in the context of what the school needs. The coach is charged with keeping the principal focused on these areas to accelerate improvement.

Typically, coaches are experienced, mid-career principals, some of whom are New Leaders themselves. The program looks for passionate, insistent principals who are up-to-date with current practices and who have led high-performing schools themselves. New Leaders for New Schools is developing an 18-month certification model for its coaches. There are six training courses for coaches: 1) the coaching cycle; 2) coaching strategies; 3) coaching skills; 4) rigorous, data-driven instruction; 5) secondary literacy; and 6) school culture. As a result of this coursework, coaches are expected to have the coaching skills and the content knowledge relating to key practices that drive student achievement gains in schools. For New Leaders for New Schools, the leading indicators of coach effectiveness are the development of the individual leader, the institutionalization of school practices, and the improvement of student achievement gains.

The Coaching Plan provides structure to the coaching relationship and is based on a leadership assessment of the New Leader principal and a diagnostic of the school's needs. For example, a school's focus might be implementing an interim assessment cycle and the New Leader's personal leadership development focus is building relationships with the faculty to develop urgency and commitment for data-driven instruction. The coach might provide support by co-facilitating a meeting with the leadership team to self-assess the school against the Data-Driven Instruction Rubric; debriefing the meeting with the New Leader; and observing a data meeting between the New Leader and faculty and providing feedback afterward. The coach consistently matches his/her coaching strategies with the context and uses observation, questioning, feedback, and commitment to next steps to build the capacity of the New Leader to direct the work without support going forward.

Training Coaches

The **NYC Leadership Academy's** unique facilitative, competency-based coaching model focuses on enabling participants to strengthen their school leadership skills within the context of school improvement work, as measured against behaviorally based performance standards. Coaches are there to help principals build their capacity to lead schools; they help them plan difficult conversations, design appropriate professional development sessions, analyze and diagnose student data, and make action plans going forward. Their job is to ask the right questions to help the principal be reflective and keep the important school issues front and center. If the situation warrants, coaches may step in and be directive. If, for example, a principal is about to make a job-risking decision, the coach might intervene in order to help the leader make a good decision or at least be aware of the choice he or she is making. In general, however, the coach is a behind-the-scenes facilitator.

Previously, the Leadership Academy placed a priority on hiring coaches with strong facilitative skills, regardless of their backgrounds. The program has come to realize that the best coaches are grounded in the principal experience and understand the work of a school leader, including how to navigate the district and a bureaucracy (procurement, teacher's union, etc.). Now the Leadership Academy trains its coaches (mostly retired, effective principals) on the facilitative skills: how to ask good questions, assess where principals are struggling, and guide inexperienced leaders to logical decisions. The program also uses training time to ensure that coaches are up-to-date with the latest school trends (standards, data-driven instruction), research, and the district's approach.

New coaches are affected in the following ways:
▷ Receive two to three days of experiential training
▷ For two days, an expert on staff joins on a school visit with the coach to observe, model, and debrief the conversations
▷ First assignments supervised by staff

Returning coaches receive a different training including:
▷ Three times a year a supervisor joins in a coaching conversation and gives the coach feedback afterward
▷ Depending on the needs of the coach, single-day training is provided to improve skills or provide new information. If more intensive support is required, quarterly full-day training may be offered
▷ Peer coaches join in on coaching sessions three times a year (this allows coaches to see other styles and approaches)

Coaches do regular school visits at least every two weeks and are also available by phone or email as needed. Supervisors monitor the work of the coaches and hold them accountable for principal success. It is expected that coaches struggling to help their principals be good leaders will contact their supervisor to raise particular issues and address them jointly. The school quality review and the progress report from the New York City Department of Education give insight into the effectiveness of the principal. The supervisor meets with every coach to review these documents and talk about how to keep moving the individual and the school forward. Successful coaches create trusting, collaborative coaching environments that enable participants to engage in critical and targeted reflection on their practice and encourage new principals to go farther to accelerate student outcomes.

EVALUATING THE IMPACT OF COACHES

While RLA programs are investing in coaching, they admit it can be difficult to measure the impact. Most are taking the approach that coaches should be held accountable for and evaluated on the development of the individual and the success of the school. The coach's job is to be a strong sounding board for the principal, building capacity, providing support, and acting as a thought partner on the tough issues. RLA programs each have their own ways of monitoring coaches' performance, and all are willing to release coaches who are not contributing to the principal's ability to develop or move a school forward.

Additionally, some RLA programs expect their coaches to take a long-term view of the principal's career goals and the school's leadership needs. For example, at the **University of Illinois at Chicago** (UIC), the coach pushes the principal to think ahead about how long he or she wants to remain in this school, what a next challenge might be, and how to plan for succession. With this career planning and counseling support, the coach has two goals. One goal is to help engage and keep the principal moving forward in the right kind of school setting that makes use of his/her talents and skills. (The program also uses the opportunity to groom its most effective principals to become UIC faculty and coaches by engaging them in conference presentations and using them as adjunct faculty to deliver program coursework or to prepare for increased district leadership.) The second goal is to move beyond principal support to managing support across schools and retaining top talent in the system.

Access to Experts

In addition to matching principals with coaches, RLA programs tend to have a wide network of experts that they or their principals can call on as needed. For example, **NYC Leadership Academy** has specialists with deep knowledge of particular issues. If a principal needs help establishing operational systems within the school, such as master high school scheduling or attendance data systems, the program can call in an expert. **New Leaders for New Schools** principals call on a data-driven instruction specialist as needed. The program also retains consultants with expertise in evaluation, staff development, and school culture who can be called on for observations and advice.

Ongoing Professional Development

Another form of support and continued learning, in addition to coaching and expert assistance, is ongoing professional development workshops. Many RLA programs may provide targeted training opportunities ranging from a full-day, on-site professional development for school administrators to off-site conferences, to a series of workshops held over the course of the school year. Topics presented are relevant to new principals and might include data-driven instruction and the formative assessment cycle, community engagement, or other topics pertinent to first-year principals. These workshops sometimes include principals' leadership teams to help spread the practices more broadly, give the principal reinforcement, and develop a shared language and understanding of approach.

For example, the **NYC Leadership Academy** offers workshops on an as-needed basis. One popular topic is deep data analysis. The Leadership Academy has a data expert on hand who helps the coach to gather the relevant information and plan the session. The coach then leads the principal, the cabinet, and the inquiry team in reviewing state test data, interim assessments, and student work to help them to recognize patterns and diagnose student needs. The team is given an assignment of thinking through the instructional implications of the data analysis and formulating a plan, which the group then discusses at the follow-up workshop.

Gwinnett County Public Schools offers an annual Quality-Plus Leader Academy Summer Leadership Conference for school and district leaders. (See *Appendix F* for more information on the conference.) The district also offers just-in-time training on key topics such as monitoring and updating the local school plan; evaluating the impact of actions taken to improve student achievement; and selecting and retaining quality personnel. (A fact sheet on the Quality-Plus Leader Academy Just-in-Time Training is included in *Appendix F*.)

The **Long Beach Unified School District** supports the transition of principals into new school sites with a Change of Principal (COP) Workshop conducted during the summer, prior to the start of school. The workshop is held on-site and includes a diverse group representing the teaching staff and classified employees (not administrators). The session is facilitated by a school coach, or other principal, and focuses on gaining insights from the group about what is working at the school and what could be improved. The incoming principal is introduced at the beginning of the session in order to create a connection with the staff. The discussion amongst the group is conducted without the principal in the room and gives staff the opportunity to express their thoughts about the change in leadership. At the conclusion of the workshop, the new principal receives both an oral and a written report with information on school processes that need attention or require continued support in order to ease his/her transition into the school.

New principals are also assigned a new principal coach. These coaches are current principals who work at the same level (elementary, middle, etc.) and who are recognized as excellent principals by their supervisor. New principals and their coaches hold weekly phone sessions, and meet face-to-face at the new principals' schools twice each month to conduct instructional walkthroughs, focus on problem-solving, and to give attention to the priorities identified in the COP Workshops. A mid-year staff survey provides additional feedback data to the new principal and his/her coach regarding progress on the COP priorities. Coaching support continues through the second year of the principalship.

Peer Cohort Coaching

There is general agreement in the field that more needs to be done to retain outstanding principals. The principalship is an isolated job that does not regularly allow for connections and collaborative learning with peers. Having a network where sitting principals can openly share problems, problem-solve together, and give feedback can be very powerful in building instructional leadership skills.

SEE PAGE 194

Learn more in Appendix F.

SEE PAGE 194

Learn more in Appendix F.

The RLA experience indicates that principals are hungry for the opportunity to collaborate with peers to deeply unpack and respond to shared challenges.

The RLA experience indicates that principals are hungry for the opportunity to collaborate with peers to deeply unpack and respond to shared challenges. Once a strong network is in place and relationships are formed, individuals often turn to their colleagues to get advice and counsel as issues arise. The ongoing stimulation and support from peers may actually help not only with effectiveness but also with principal tenure, which can be an issue in schools that have a history of low performance.

EXAMPLE

The **School Leaders Network** (SLN) serves school leaders with a collaborative coaching model. SLN regional networks are made up of self-selected mostly experienced principals from traditional school districts or CMOs who work in underserved areas. These leaders meet collaboratively with a SLN Facilitator to develop a strong sense of professional community, and accelerate their instructional leadership skills by deeply investigating a problem of instructional practice together. This investigation models a transformative, problem-solving inquiry approach that leaders take back to their schools and incorporate as part of their own leadership practice. Networks convene monthly after school to best maximize the time and needs of the school leader. The SLN model is based on a three-tiered experience that builds a strong collaborative community; then focuses on accelerating instructional leadership skills; and finally the cohort, under the guidance of the trained facilitator, holds the group accountable for transferring this work back to the schools for increased teacher capacity.

SLN uses skilled facilitators to structure the conversations and push the group to solve common problems of practice together. Problems may include topics such as:

▷ Promoting higher-level thinking for lifelong learning: What kinds of questions are teachers asking students? What kinds of questions are students asking teachers and one another? How might we categorize these questions and foster higher-level questioning to increase student achievement as measured by a selected instrument?
▷ Increasing rigor to boost student achievement: What is happening between the teacher and the students in classrooms where rigorous learning occurs? What is missing in classrooms with less rigorous learning?
▷ Differentiated teaching strategies: What strategies do teachers use when delivering high-quality differentiated instruction? What is evidence of differentiated tasks? What do students report learning during differentiated activities?

(A sample network meeting plan from School Leaders Network can be found in *Appendix F.*)

SEE PAGE 194

Learn more
in Appendix F.

Principals are pushed to think systemically and establish long-range goals without getting sidetracked by smaller problems. As a result of their network interactions, SLN principals point to improvement in the following leadership practices:

▷ Adoption of new leadership tools
▷ Ability to take on instructional and human capital issues more confidently
▷ Enhanced leadership of teacher learning communities
▷ Increased use of inquiry-based school study
▷ Improved classroom observation practice

Support for Whole Schools

In general, RLA programs understand that the "heroic" single-leader model is not enough and help their principals develop other adults in the building, especially the school leadership team. Coaching can be used to help build a successful school culture and drive high levels of performance that are sustainable beyond one particular leader. RLA programs may also offer professional development for principals and their leadership teams.

In order to help ensure the success of the entire school, some RLA programs are choosing to engage other leaders within the school. For example, at the **University of Illinois at Chicago** (UIC), the coach not only supports the principal, but is also very involved in strengthening the skills of the entire leadership team. While the coach does not attend all leadership team meetings, he or she does help the principal to set goals and plan the leadership work needed to accomplish those goals. For example, the coach may ask the principal to reflect on the roles of the department teams and the grade-level teams in moving student achievement; to consider how the leadership team can establish a culture of high expectations in the school on a day-to-day basis; to determine the best way to communicate and build a relationship with the local school council, etc. The UIC coach seeks to develop the leadership skills of the group as a whole. The coach and principal then work together to facilitate and monitor the work of the individuals on the leadership team as a way of moving the school toward its goals.

Other programs are using diagnostic instruments to identify school needs and using coaching or other supports to help leaders move the school forward. **New Leaders for New Schools** uses a school-wide diagnostic tool derived from its Urban Excellence Framework™ (UEF). The tool assesses the school against the 18 UEF levers and identifies the right work for the school by identifying the lever(s) that will drive dramatic student achievement gains. The leadership team members participate in the diagnostic process and own the resulting action plan equally with the New Leader principal and the coach. New Leaders for New Schools has also developed a set of leadership team standards defining what a leadership team should know and be able to do. Using a self-assessment tool, the leadership team members measure their progress toward the standards. The coach and New Leader refer to these standards throughout the school year to increase the capabilities of the leadership team.

To enable school and regional leaders to measure leading indicators of school health and diagnose school needs, **KIPP** developed metrics and surveys that measure student, family, and staff perceptions. The Healthy Schools Initiative defines characteristics of healthy schools that go beyond student outcomes to include school leadership and organizational systems, talent, culture and climate, and teaching and learning. The Healthy Schools framework:

▷ Creates a shared language for describing, measuring, and reflecting upon school and regional health
▷ Defines health in a broad, inclusive way that is reflective of KIPP's values and mission—including a focus on what it takes to truly prepare students for success in college and beyond
▷ Guides data collection, with the goal of gathering and sharing the best possible data for making strategic decisions in schools and regions
▷ Deepens understanding of school performance and points to factors most impacting results
▷ Helps identify schools and regions that may have promising practices to share

KIPP's definition of school health includes a focus on both the student outcomes expected in KIPP schools, as well as the leading indicators that drive these outcomes. Specifically, it is through excellent practice in leadership and organizational systems, culture and climate, human capital, and academics that student attainment is achieved. This consistent framework gives KIPP School Leaders a tool for cross-school comparisons and allows them to learn from and connect to peers within the network who have demonstrated effective practices. It also provides objective data points on issues such as leadership development and bench strength, staff recruitment and retention, and instructional strategies that principals and coaches can use for strategic planning purposes. Schools that participate are supplied with performance dashboards, which summarize their data results in comparison with other schools in the network on an annual basis.

KIPP also has a long-standing contract with a third-party outside provider (that pre-dates the Healthy Schools Initiative) to conduct on-site evaluations of each KIPP school every two years. The review teams, which also include KIPP Foundation staff and a principal peer from within the network, spend two-and-a-half days visiting classrooms, attending meetings, conducting interviews, and reviewing documents to collect evidence on leading indicators of school effectiveness. As a result, each school is given a report that outlines strengths as well as two to three priority areas that will most affect the health and performance of their schools. The reviews are both an evaluation of principal effectiveness and a source of support in that they provide valuable information about school performance, an outside perspective on how to keep the school moving forward, and recommended action steps to get started.

RLA programs are all mission-driven and therefore, they care about placement and support to ensure that principals are placed in right-fit schools, are supported as they start the work, and have the right district conditions to maximize their chances of success.

Creating Improved Conditions at the District or State Level

A few RLA programs are supporting the work of school leaders by engaging the district (and sometimes the state) to ensure that it creates the environment and conditions to help principals be effective in their jobs. District policies, practices, and infrastructure all affect principals and can either hinder or help them in transforming struggling schools.

Some district policy or practice changes are straightforward but can have a significant impact. For example, as mentioned earlier, simply hiring principals earlier in the year allows school leaders to engage with their staffs and make plans, rather than coming in under someone else's plan and vision. In addition, too often, school leaders lack the authority and autonomy to hire staff, manage their budget, implement curriculum, and/or arrange the school schedule. Giving principals decision-making power is critical to their success. Districts also need to ensure that principals, as instructional leaders, have data systems, including benchmark/formative tests, and access to timely results. More and more, RLA programs are clearly defining the conditions and structures that impact principal effectiveness. In some cases, programs are directly engaging with districts and states to review their existing policies and practices and establish the school-level supports needed.

EXAMPLE

Since its inception in 2000, **New Leaders for New Schools** has conducted research on the impact of their principals on schools and has consistently found that principal effectiveness is dependent on having aligned conditions in the district. New Leaders has therefore committed to improving district (and state) alignment in order to increase the likelihood that its graduates will be successful on the job. First, New Leaders believes it is extremely important that the person the principal reports to within the district has aligned beliefs, shares the sense of urgency for student gains, and understands that significant changes in practice within a school are required in order to drive gains. Principals that have managers who share a common goal and are supported in their work are more likely to have higher job satisfaction and longer retention. Second, New Leaders for New Schools seeks out district partners that have policies and practices in place to drive principal effectiveness and retention, including significant decision-making authority for principals on staffing, budget, and professional development practices.

In order to ensure the best possible district alignment with these beliefs, New Leaders for New Schools conducts a city selection process to determine with which school districts they will engage. District partners are required to sign a memorandum of understanding (MOU) that defines the conditions and policy changes that the program and the district agree to put in place as part of the partnership. As one example, the district agrees to move up its placement timeline to ensure that principals (and teachers) are in place early enough that they have time to diagnose the needs of the school and prepare for the year ahead. This is especially important in turnaround situations. Finally, the MOU may include defining principal performance standards with an evaluation system aligned to those standards. New Leaders for New Schools conducts an annual district partnership review to make sure that both partners are following through on their commitments.

> Post-program principal coaching is different from coaching during residency in that newly placed principals need more intense support on a wider range of issues. No longer are they "trying on the job" with a segment of teachers and students, they are the school leaders responsible for every aspect of school management and instructional leadership.

In addition to establishing non-negotiable criteria when engaging with partner districts, New Leaders for New Schools has taken on a broader policy support role with some of its partner states and districts. Program staff members find that many states and districts would like to improve their systems alignment but need additional capacity and technical support to enact policy and practice changes. New Leaders for New Schools has launched a consulting team that provides the extra staff capacity needed to help partner states and districts coordinate policies and practices into a coherent and cohesive approach.

University of Virginia's Darden/Curry Partnership for Leaders in Education (PLE) engages a "district shepherd" (typically the deputy superintendent) who visits turnaround schools where program graduates are sitting principals on a weekly basis to provide support and resources. Principals can be more effective in turning around low-performing schools if they have backing and support at the district level on issues such as:

- Ability to hire new staff (or at least greater flexibility relative to hiring and replacement)
- Clear, fast timelines for results, with strong gains expected in year one
- Job-embedded professional development aligned with data-driven decision-making
- Regular school audits assessing mutually agreed-upon leading indicators for success
- Flexibility in the length of the school day or school year
- Quick turnaround of data, including district-wide formative assessments
- Comprehensive principal and teacher evaluation system, with leaders held accountable for results
- Co-development of aligned school and district strategic plans
- District and state alignment on school reporting and accountability criteria

In one of PLE's partner districts, there is a "Rapid Response Team" dedicated to ensuring that problems surfaced by turnaround principals are attended to within 24 hours. The PLE program's goal is to build the capacity of the district shepherd so that the support can be sustained beyond the length of the program-district contract.

Although the level of engagement at the district and state levels varies by program, RLA programs are aware of the importance of aligning resources and support in order to help principals more easily gain momentum and leverage. Not all RLA programs are proactive in trying to change district practice and policy. But they are all very clear about their program missions: to train principals who can lead school transformations and improve student outcomes. By being upfront about their goals and the fact that student needs come first, RLA programs seek to clear a path for their graduates to do the hard work.

Evaluation and Assessment

RLA programs are all mission-driven and therefore, they care a lot about placement and support to ensure that principals are placed in right-fit schools, are supported as they start the work, and have the right district conditions to maximize their chances of success. Most importantly, they want to know about the impact of their graduates once in schools: Are the principals successful in dramatically improving student achievement? (See the *Program Evaluation* chapter for more on this.) Have they strengthened the effectiveness of the school and its key components (e.g. instruction, culture, operations)? Do they stay in their jobs long enough to make a sustainable difference? If they leave a job, did they set their school up well for succession and remain in the field to continue to have impact (e.g. Assistant Superintendent, Principal Coach, etc.)?

SEE PAGE 116

Learn more in the Program Evaluation chapter.

In addition to student achievement measures and leading indicators, some RLA programs track the following indicators of success in terms of the support they provide:

▷ Number of placements (principals and assistant principals) and the percentage of graduates placed immediately and within two years of program completion
▷ The retention of those principalships over two, three, and five years
▷ Changes in school practices in the first year of the principalship
▷ Improvements in leadership abilities in the first year of the principalship
▷ Principals' satisfaction with residency year and first-year principal supports

COST AND RESOURCE ALLOCATION CONSIDERATIONS

Significant staff time is involved in successful principal placement and the follow-up support services, which can extend a year or more. Programs need to be mindful of staff time involved in providing individualized support to all graduates and determine the cost-benefit ratio of the various options:

▷ Staff to work with district on placement
▷ One-on-one coaching support
▷ Workshops and other professional development opportunities
▷ Peer support
▷ School-level support
▷ District-level influence and engagement

Lessons Learned

As highlighted throughout this chapter, RLA programs take seriously their commitment to place high-quality school leaders in high-need schools. They carefully assess and match their graduates to schools that could most benefit from their skills, knowledge, and dispositions. Then RLA programs put in place a system of support specifically designed to help first-year (and beyond) principals succeed on the job by insisting on academic improvement. RLA programs posit that:

1 *The more dependable and accurate your program's recommendations and assessments are, the more likely your program will become an integral part of the matching/placement process with district and CMO partners.*

2 *Supporting graduates and preparing them for the placement process can make a big difference in placements and opportunities.* Working with district and CMO partners to determine school leadership needs early is important, starting several months before the hiring process begins.

3 *The work of transforming schools is really tough and first-year leaders need support at various levels*, ranging from the individual to the school level and even including influencing the district/state to purposefully enact policies and practices to increase their chances of success.

4 *Coaching can be immensely helpful to new principals but RLA members also value networks and peer groups*, which can help principals build skills for themselves and meaningfully collaborate with one another.

5 *Principals are able to be most effective and accelerate change in districts and CMOs with aligned conditions, practices and policies.*

6 There is a lot more we need to learn about what supports principals need to build their consistent capacity for success. *Programs need to be set up in such a way as to collect, track, and analyze various kinds of data to make strong recommendations on principal placement and to drive high-quality supports for principals.*

A Look Ahead: Program Evaluation

As highlighted throughout this chapter, RLA programs expend significant resources in order to prepare their principals to stand on their own as effective leaders driving student growth. RLA programs are committed to measuring the effectiveness of their graduates and their work in this area is discussed in the next chapter, *Program Evaluation.*

Program Evaluation

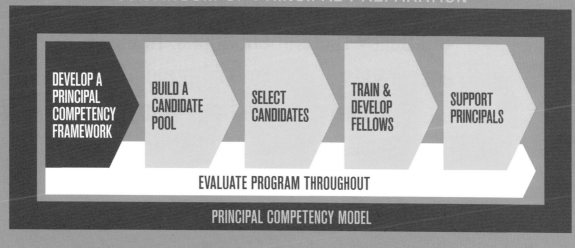

CONTINUUM OF PRINCIPAL PREPARATION

DEVELOP A PRINCIPAL COMPETENCY FRAMEWORK

BUILD A CANDIDATE POOL

SELECT CANDIDATES

TRAIN & DEVELOP FELLOWS

SUPPORT PRINCIPALS

EVALUATE PROGRAM THROUGHOUT

PRINCIPAL COMPETENCY MODEL

6

6 **PROGRAM EVALUATION** | The mission of the RLA programs is to dramatically improve student outcomes and close achievement gaps. They rely on an ongoing data feedback loop to strengthen their own models, and in a departure from other school leader preparation programs, they ultimately hold themselves accountable for the on-the-job performance of their graduates, including student achievement results, despite limitations in the available data. While this commitment to tracking graduates and their impacts on schools and students once on the job is a shift in practice, other programs are likely to fall in line in light of one of the U.S. Department of Education's Race to the Top policy recommendations. Race to the Top encourages states to hold principal preparation programs accountable for principal-effectiveness measures, especially student achievement results. This new focus on outcomes will have implications for the field as a whole, driving more programs to track the placement and performance of graduates.

The Evaluation Plan

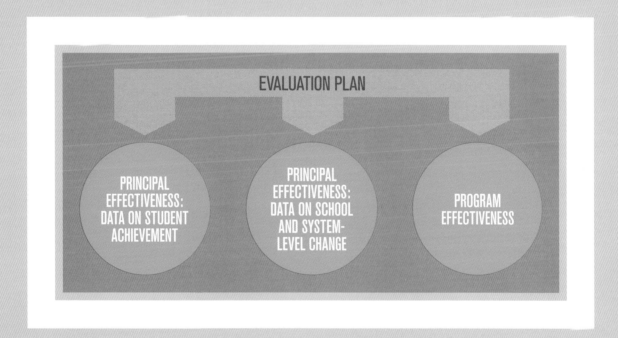

This chapter is not intended to be a how-to guide on evaluation. Evaluation design and analysis is a serious and complicated endeavor. Instead, the goal of this chapter is to highlight the RLA emphasis on evaluation as an important component of principal preparation. **RLA programs endeavor to measure the impact of their training and development on the growth of their principals, as a way to continuously improve** their offerings and strengthen the effectiveness of their graduates. **They also evaluate the impact of their principals on their schools and students**, specifically in the areas of **teacher effectiveness and student achievement outcomes**.

There are data challenges inherent in this work and yet, each of the RLA programs is deeply committed to capturing and using data to evaluate efforts. They use the best available, public data and push their own capacity for collection and analysis. RLA programs that have done the most in-depth evaluation work have engaged third-party evaluators, and some have negotiated with districts to access more robust data than is generally available. While, most RLA programs are working hard at evaluation, none feel they have it figured out fully. We present this component of the principal preparation continuum as a work in progress and hope that the reader comes away with a better understanding about the importance of and challenges involved in collecting and interpreting data.

Evaluating the Impact of the Program on Their Principals

RLA programs use evaluation to discern the impact of their training and development on the growth of each of their matriculating leaders. Program leaders hold themselves accountable for systematically graduating effective leaders, and they use data to understand and improve the continuum of experiences they offer to continuously strengthen their models.

Specifically, programs are interested in understanding which aspects of their models are most effective in helping prepare principals for the challenges of the job. This can be difficult to determine because these programs use rigorous selection processes that winnow out those who do not demonstrate a certain set of skills, knowledge, and dispositions upon entry. Are the trainees good simply because of the qualities and talents they had upon entry, or did what they learned through an RLA program experience improve their effectiveness? Isolating the effects of the training from the selection process (and a myriad of other factors) is no easy task. But RLA programs, like the schools and districts they serve, are committed to measuring their own value-add.

> There are data challenges inherent in this work and yet, each of the RLA programs is deeply committed to capturing and using data to evaluate efforts.

To understand the relative strengths and weaknesses of their delivery models and design, RLA programs collect and monitor data on their graduates throughout the program period, starting as early as selection. (See evaluation sections of the *Selecting Candidates, Training and Developing Fellows*, and *Supporting Principals* chapters.) They also reach out to their alumni and instructors/mentors to collect feedback on the preparation and support provided by the program. Surveys, interviews, focus groups, and observations in the field all serve to inform programs about a principal's effectiveness and the implications for program design.

Learn more in the Selecting Candidates, Training and Developing Fellows, and Supporting Principals chapters.

Types of data collected by RLA programs include:

▷ Student achievement results—value-added data preferred (principal efficacy data also informs program efficacy)
▷ Progress: Fellow and principal progress on competencies
▷ Feedback:
  ▶ Participant feedback (during training and development and post-completion), including coursework, instructors, coaching, mentor-principals, and residency
  ▶ Instructor, coach, and mentor-principal feedback
  ▶ Supervisor or other district staff feedback
  ▶ Principal surveys (post-induction)
▷ Completion, placement, and retention rates:
  ▶ Program completion rates
  ▶ Placement rates in principalships, assistant principalships, central district leadership, etc.
  ▶ Retention rates within the system over time (3+ years) compared with other new principals
▷ Cost per participant

New Leaders for New Schools, like other RLA programs, is looking at the impact of its principals on schools and using that information to strengthen its selection process and training components. New Leaders for New Schools conducts in-depth investigations of school-level practices and leadership actions at work in *dramatically gaining schools*. Program staff members visit schools, interview personnel, and interact with staff to identify key practices and actions of the principals, their graduates. New Leaders for New Schools then uses these findings to amend their training and development coursework, adjust the residency experience, and focus the coaching component to help fellows grow in these important areas. This realignment of services and supports is ongoing.

Evaluating the Impact of the Program's Principals on School Outcomes

RLA programs monitor their principals to determine their impact on school outcomes, the most important of which is student achievement. To do so, one of the first commitments RLA programs make is to track their graduates' placement. The focus on knowing and following principals' work post-graduation is an innovation in the field. (Many traditional principal preparation programs do not expect their graduates to immediately enter the principalship, nor do they track their graduates' placements or results.) And even this simple placement data can be difficult to gather. Programs that work closely with a district, such as the **NYC Leadership Academy**, which partners with the New York City Department of Education, may not have access to district principal placement data. Or the data may be outdated and inaccurate. As principals move to different schools over time, longitudinal data is particularly challenging. As a result, the Leadership Academy, like the other RLA programs, has had to heavily invest in developing its own data system to track this information. Significant personnel time is dedicated to following up with alumni to confirm school placements and keep up-to-date records on file.

One of the most important jobs of the principal is setting a high-expectations culture and providing instructional leadership to support the teaching staff. Principals who can put effective teachers in every classroom are likely to see, and sustain, student gains. However, evaluating a principal's ability to build teachers' capacity and manage human capital within a school is not easy.

RLA programs therefore want to evaluate the overall health of a school by monitoring multiple measures that correlate to student achievement. RLA programs typically construct a data dashboard that includes not only student results, but other important and related data to help programs determine if a school is heading in the right direction.

The following are some measures that RLA programs might include in their data dashboards:

> Program leaders hold themselves accountable for systematically graduating effective leaders, and they use data to understand and improve the continuum of experiences they offer to continuously strengthen their models.

- Student achievement indicators
- School environment indicators (e.g., attendance rates, misconduct levels including suspensions)
- Teacher satisfaction with principal support, absences and performance ratings, retention/turnover, improved teacher impact on student achievement
- District surveys of students, teachers, and parents (many of the large cities such as New York, Chicago, and Baltimore allow these data to be downloaded and analyzed)
- Principal evaluations (e.g., qualitative reports by teachers/mentor-principals, etc.)

Getting Good Principal Effectiveness Data

Student achievement data are critical in determining teacher and principal effectiveness. However, the quality and accessibility of the data vary widely across districts and states, and by grade level and subject. Programs need to determine whether they will rely on *value-added* or *absolute* data or both and whether their unit of change will be at the *student level* or the *school level*. These are all important and complicated decisions with trade-offs. Statisticians are working hard to determine how best to use student achievement data to measure teacher and principal effectiveness.

RLA programs point to a number of overall challenges inherent in tracking, monitoring, and analyzing achievement data relating to principal effectiveness, including that:

The landscape of assessments within states is ever-changing. It is not unusual for states to make changes to their state assessments or the cut scores (percentage of correct responses needed to achieve a passing score) or standards, which make it difficult for programs to measure results over the long term.

Many grades and subjects do not have publically reported test data. There is limited data at the high school level. Because federal accountability policy has only required testing in one grade level within the four-year high school experience (making student-level, year-to-year value-added calculations impossible), programs necessarily need to capture other data points to assess principal effectiveness. Further, data such as graduation rates are often not considered "clean and final" until far into the following school year.

Attaining student-level data and conducting value-added analysis can be complicated and expensive.

Comparisons across geographies are difficult. The complexity of state-level standards hampers the ability of programs to make cross-state comparisons between schools.

Principal tenure information is not made publicly available. This is a variable that programs often would like to control when making comparisons across schools. Programs can monitor their own graduates but do not have easy access to tenure information in comparison schools. For programs working across districts especially, local program sites will need to create a data system to track this information and find ways to keep tabs on graduates over time.

Data dashboards also include student achievement results, although RLA programs recognize that some of the other data points above may show improvement before test scores do. The most systematic and complete data that exist to track results are from state standardized achievement tests and RLA program evaluations uniformly use these tests, either at the school level or student level. While these are not perfect, as a direct measure of student learning gains, they are the current best measure available. The tests are not administered in every grade and they may not always cover all of the core subject areas, but they provide the most consistent look at student proficiency and growth over time that we have. In instances where programs can partner with districts to help provide the data, analysis is much easier. As states and districts make student-level data more readily available, more robust analysis will be possible by more programs.

Some of these data are publicly available and some the programs collect themselves. For example, the **NYC Leadership Academy** draws on school surveys done by the New York City Department of Education that report on the degree to which teachers feel they understand the mission of the school, how satisfied they are with the support they get from their principal, and how much they use data to inform instruction. Students are asked whether they have an adult to go to in their school if needed. Parents are asked about communication with the school and openness to their involvement. The Leadership Academy uses these learning environment surveys as a source of information on how effective a principal is in establishing a healthy school environment.

As mentioned in earlier chapters, **KIPP's** Healthy Schools Initiative examines the on-the-ground practices and conditions that make a school healthy. Leading indicators include leadership and organizational systems, human capital, culture and climate, academics, college preparatory supports, and operations. These data allow KIPP leaders to critically assess the performance of their schools, identify effective practices by viewing data from across the network, highlight top performers and share strategies for improvement with one another. KIPP seeks to identify the factors that most impact results, creating a feedback loop of constant improvement. (A summary of the Healthy Schools Initiative can be found on page 111 of the *Supporting Principals* chapter.)

Learn more in the Supporting Principals chapter.

SEE PAGE 111

> Specifically, programs are interested in understanding which aspects of their models are most effective in helping prepare principals for the challenges of the job.

Partnering with External Evaluators

Because gathering and analyzing this data–especially at the student level–is so complicated, a few of the most mature RLA programs have enlisted external evaluators to conduct more comprehensive and sophisticated studies, all of which include data from standardized tests but are not limited to them.

KIPP's major evaluation efforts are conducted by Mathematica Policy Research. The study design includes a quasi-experimental component (matching KIPP students with similar non-KIPP students from the surrounding districts) and an experimental component, or randomized control trial, in which lotteries of oversubscribed KIPP schools are used to identify equivalent treatment and control groups. The research questions for the study focus on understanding KIPP's impact on students in both academic and non-academic terms. In its June 2010 report, Mathematica found that "for the vast majority of KIPP schools studied, impacts on students' state assessment scores in mathematics and reading are positive, statistically significant, and educationally substantial. Estimated impacts are frequently large enough to substantially reduce race- and income-based achievement gaps within three years of entering KIPP."[13] While the focus of the study is not school leaders per se, because KIPP selects and trains its teachers and leaders, the study results certainly have implications for the program's principal preparation work.

New Leaders for New Schools is now beginning the fifth year of the RAND Corporation's multi-year study of the impact of the program, including surveys, fieldwork, and a rigorous longitudinal analysis using student-level data from all children across current districts. RAND's value-added analyses, which track individual student growth compared with that of similar children in non-New Leader-led schools, uses standard student-level indicators (demographics, prior scores, mobility, special education/English learner status) and also controls for principal tenure. RAND is able to calculate individual students' changes in achievement by controlling for prior achievement levels and characteristics, including when they were in different schools. Preliminary results indicate that students in elementary and middle schools led by New Leaders principals for at least three years are academically outpacing their peers by statistically significant margins (Martorell, Heaton, Gates, and Hamilton, 2010).[14]

The **NYC Leadership Academy** has also engaged a third-party evaluator, New York University's Institute for Education and Social Policy. In August 2009, NYU issued "The New York City Aspiring Principals Program: A School-Level Evaluation," the first systematic comparison of student outcomes in schools led by Aspiring Principals Program (APP) graduates after three years to those in comparable schools led by other new principals. The study found that APP graduates were more likely to be placed in schools where the average student performed substantially below the citywide grade-level average in English Language Arts (ELA) and mathematics before their arrival, while students in comparison schools scored approximately at the citywide grade-level average in these subjects. Nonetheless, elementary and middle schools led by APP graduates made greater gains in ELA than comparison schools, improving apace with citywide gains in ELA performance. Schools led by APP graduates also make gains in math (these gains were slightly smaller than in the comparison schools but not statistically significant).[15]

EXAMPLE

New Leaders for New Schools has created a three-pronged definition of principal effectiveness that it measures, which includes:

Student Outcomes: The principal's primary marker of success is the improvement of student achievement and a small number of additional student outcomes, such as high school graduation, college matriculation, college readiness, or attendance rates.

Teacher Effectiveness: Teacher quality is the most important in-school factor relating to student achievement. Principals drive effectiveness through their role as a human capital manager—including teacher hiring, evaluation, professional development, retention, leadership development, and dismissal—and by providing instructional leadership.

Leadership Actions: The highly effective principal makes accelerated progress in implementing the principal actions and school-wide practices that differentiate rapidly improving schools. Leadership categories that must be addressed to drive breakthrough student and teacher growth include: 1) learning and teaching; 2) building and managing a high-quality staff aligned to the school's vision of success for every student; 3) developing an achievement- and belief-based school-wide culture; 4) instituting operations and systems to support learning; and 5) modeling personal leadership that sets the tone for all student and adult relationships in the school. Each of these categories is further divided into a subset of key levers, each representing a collection of actions taken by highly effective principals.

RLA programs examine student achievement results within a school and also compare the progress of schools led by their principals with other schools, both within and outside the district. Metrics commonly tracked include:

▷ Measures of growth (can be school- or student-level, longitudinal or cohort comparison, with various controls for demographics, socioeconomic status, etc.)
▷ Absolute measures:
  ▷ Percentage of schools in top quartile of proficiency gains in the district
  ▷ Decrease in the percentage of students at lowest proficiency levels
  ▷ Percentage of program schools outperforming district/ comparable school average
  ▷ Attainment and other student performance data (e.g., graduation rates, dropout rates, credit accumulation, post-secondary entry/ completion)
▷ Performance of schools in certain categories compared with other appropriate schools (high school, elementary school, charter, new schools, small schools, schools in lowest-performing quartile of the district, etc.)

COST AND RESOURCE ALLOCATION CONSIDERATIONS

Evaluation is resource-intensive in terms of money, staff time, and elapsed time. Data, especially at the student level, can be difficult and time consuming to collect and analyze. Third-party evaluators often conduct multiple-year studies, which can be extremely expensive and involve significant coordination at the school and district level. RLA programs illustrate that the longer they have been in operation—and the more data they have to track—the more resources (usually a full-time person at minimum, and sometimes a third-party evaluator) need to be devoted to the evaluation effort.

Lessons Learned

Fortunately, there is a general trend toward improving the quality of the data available at the student and school level, and making that data more generally available. This effort will help programs to more accurately measure their own impacts on individual principals, and then the contribution of those principals in schools and on students. While there are a myriad of data limitations, at this point, RLA programs are using available data as well as they can to hold themselves accountable for the results of their graduates and to continuously improve the design and implementation of their models.

At this point, RLA members have these lessons to share:

1. While student achievement is the most important and ultimate outcome for principal preparation programs, it is equally important to capture and monitor multiple measures of success that give early indication of a school headed in the right direction before student achievement results are yielded. It is also important for a program to measure its impact on its participants to track its value-add and to improve its program.

2. A variety of data points should be monitored to ensure a complete picture of principal impact. For instance, when new practices are initiated, there may be an "implementation dip." A drop in test scores might correlate with dramatic improvements in the dropout rate, indicating not that student achievement dropped but that previously disengaged, and perhaps lower-performing, students stayed in school in greater numbers. A principal may come in with high expectations and a commitment to changing the culture and setting a serious tone, which could drive up disciplinary actions. Once those initial interventions take hold, behavior interventions are likely to decrease.

3. RLA programs, like the field as a whole, struggle to find ways to measure a principal's ability to build teacher capacity. Yet they recognize the fundamental importance of the human resources component in the success of a school. At least one RLA program is working to formally define principal effectiveness measures as tied to increased teacher effectiveness, in addition to student achievement.

4. Only sustained results, particularly when leadership is consistent for three or more years, reflect real improvement. Beware of single blips in the data. Sometimes there will be drops in test scores as new practices are implemented, but the overall health of the school may still be on a positive trajectory. Similarly, positive data spikes may not be sustainable.

Conclusion

We must do a better job of ensuring that all schools have an effective principal driving the charge to guarantee that all students get the quality teaching they need and deserve.

Throughout this document, we have attempted to capture the collective practices of the RLA programs that are on the forefront of innovation in principal preparation. These programs diligently document their results—continually adapting their models accordingly—with the ultimate goal of improving student outcomes. Our intent was to highlight their evolving thinking and lessons learned in hopes of advancing the broader field.

As has been stressed throughout, the work of the RLA members is based on leading research and a very real-time assessment of the actions of high-performing principals. The effective school leader competencies are the foundation and link between all program elements—from building a candidate pool, to selecting candidates, to developing aspiring leaders, to supporting new principals, and evaluating program and principal effectiveness. The interrelatedness of these components is key to the RLA programs' approach, as these models exist to prepare leaders who can dramatically improve student achievement.

The RLA programs have forged a new path—distinct from the more traditional methods of principal preparation. These entrepreneurial programs are dedicated to preparing and supporting quality school leadership, and tracking their results in schools. They apply the following theory of action: by increasing the number of effective principals, they will, in turn, ensure successive years of quality teaching for students, and as a result, will improve and sustain student achievement.

We applaud their efforts and are optimistic that with the focus on rigorous selection, training, and development, and support by more programs across the country, a new generation of school leaders will be better prepared to meet the challenges of a 21st-century school system. However, it is important to note that even if we had perfect principal training models, the work would not be done. Districts, states, and other stakeholders must do a better job of aligning strategies, systems, and programs if we expect this next generation of school leaders to be successful, particularly in turning around low-achieving schools.

Principal preparation—and the parallel efforts of aligning systems and supports—is not easy work. But it is critical that we find top-quality candidates, invest in them, and create much more supportive work conditions if we expect them to be successful in tackling the challenging work of improving and running our nation's neediest schools.

We know that, second only to classroom instruction, school leadership is the most important school-based variable affecting student achievement. The school leader sets the tone and tenor of the whole school and affects the quality of the teaching staff. We must do a better job of ensuring that all schools have an effective principal driving the charge to guarantee that all students get the quality teaching they need and deserve.

RLA Program
Summaries

Gwinnett County Public Schools' Quality-Plus Leader Academy

Located just outside Atlanta, Gwinnett County, a growing school district, enrolls 160,000 students and has more than 22,000 employees. As Georgia's largest school system and the 13th largest in the country, Gwinnett County Public Schools (GCPS) values leaders who have the skills and training to lead world-class schools to increased levels of academic achievement for all students. Because of the changing demographics in its schools, school leaders must be knowledgeable about instruction, should articulate the school's vision and mission, and promote a positive school environment in an era of accountability.

Recognizing the importance of effective school leaders, Gwinnett County launched the Quality-Plus Leader Academy in 2007 to create as many as 60 new principals to lead the 37 new schools that will open in Gwinnett by 2014. The goal of the academy is to train and develop future school principals, with a curriculum created and developed by school system leaders.

Gwinnett's program recruits principal candidates from the district's teaching and administrative ranks and then provides a comprehensive year-long training program, led by GCPS division heads, that covers such topics as curriculum, assessment and instruction, budgeting and finance, operations management, and community relations. The program also includes two 25-day residency experiences with successful principals and ongoing support once a candidate is placed in the district. Currently, there are 20 members in the Quality-Plus Leader Academy Aspiring Principal Program. All candidates are current assistant principals with leadership certificates.

Gwinnett County Public Schools is one of five districts in the running for the 2010 Broad Prize for Urban Education and was a finalist in 2009. The prize honors urban school districts making the greatest progress in America in raising student achievement.

Knowledge Is Power Program (KIPP) School Leadership Program

KIPP, which started in 1994, and is headquartered in San Francisco, CA, is a national network of free, open-enrollment, college-preparatory public schools with a track record of preparing students in underserved communities for success in college and in life. There are currently 82 KIPP schools in 19 states and the District of Columbia serving more than 21,000 students. Eighty percent of KIPP students are from low-income families and eligible for the federal free and reduced-price meals program, and 90 percent are African American or Latino. Nationally, more than 90 percent of KIPP middle school students have gone on to college-preparatory high schools, and more than 85 percent of KIPP alumni have gone on to college.

In 2000, the nonprofit KIPP Foundation began training prospective principals to replicate the success of the two original KIPP academies in Houston and the South Bronx. Over the past eight years, KIPP has trained more than 80 acting principals through the KIPP School Leadership Program.

The KIPP School Leadership Program has two primary fellowships for opening a new KIPP school: a year-long Fisher Fellowship and a two-year Miles Family Fellowship.

FOR MORE INFORMATION

Contact Glenn Pethel, Executive Director of Leadership Development, or visit: www.gwinnett.k12.ga.us.

FOR MORE INFORMATION

Contact Kelly Wright, Senior Learning Officer, KIPP Foundation, or visit: www.kipp.org.

- The Fisher Fellowship offers candidates (who typically have five years of teaching experience) a year-long program that prepares them to open a new KIPP school. This fellowship includes intensive summer coursework in an academic setting, residencies at KIPP schools, and individualized coaching from experienced KIPP staff. The 2009-10 Fisher Fellowship cohort includes 15 fellows.
- The Miles Family Fellowship provides selected participants (who typically have at least three years of teaching experience) with a two-year pathway to becoming a KIPP school leader. These fellows receive a year of support and leadership experience while teaching in a KIPP school. After successfully completing the Miles Family Fellowship program, candidates will be considered for the year-long Fisher Fellowship in order to prepare them to open a new KIPP school. The 2009-10 Miles Family Fellowship cohort includes 11 fellows.

The KIPP Foundation was recently chosen as a winner in the U.S. Department of Education's Investing in Innovation, or i3, competition. Using the award, KIPP will train 1,000 new school leaders and will double over five years the number of students its charter schools serve—from 29,000 to 55,000.

Long Beach Unified School District

The Long Beach Unified School District (LBUSD) educates 86,000 students in 93 public schools in the cities of Long Beach, Lakewood, Signal Hill, and Avalon on Catalina Island. The third-largest school district in California, it serves the most diverse large city in the United States, with dozens of languages spoken by local students.

The district has a "grow your own" approach to leadership, with nearly all school leaders developed internally. Between 2002 and 2009, only four out of 69 new principals were recruited from outside the district. The Aspiring Principal Program takes 12 to 15 high-performing leaders (assistant principals or other leaders who are not in the classroom) annually, based in part on principal recommendations. Selected participants do extensive summer coursework, followed by additional coursework during the school year while they participate in leadership internships or mentorships that enable them to shadow a high-performing principal throughout the school year while serving in their current capacity as assistant principal. Once placed in schools, new principals participate in the New Principal Induction Program, which includes a change-of-principal workshop, followed by personal coaching and professional development aligned to school and personal needs.

LBUSD in 2003 was named a national winner of the Broad Prize for Urban Education, recognizing America's best urban school system for increasing student achievement. The district also has been a five-time finalist for the prize.

FOR MORE INFORMATION

Contact Kristi Kahl, Director of Research, or visit: www.lbschools.net.

New Leaders for New Schools

New Leaders for New Schools, based in New York, focuses on producing exceptional leaders with the skills to dramatically improve school performance and drive educational excellence on a national scale. Through its rigorous selection process, intensive training program, and ongoing support, New Leaders for New Schools provides a pathway for current and former educators to become outstanding principals of urban public schools.

In 2001, NLNS trained and supported 13 aspiring principals in Chicago, New York City, and the San Francisco Bay Area. In just 9 years, the program has grown to train and support more than 640 New Leaders principals across 12 urban centers. Competition is high for New Leaders slots; the selectivity rate is less than 7 percent.

Summer Foundations is a rigorous four-week training institute for New Leaders residents from across the nation. Taught by outstanding educators and national education and business leaders, the program focuses on developing instructional and organizational leadership skills. After completing this training institute, leaders begin a year-long, full-time, paid residency in an urban public school working alongside a mentor-principal. With the support of a New Leaders for New Schools coach, residents are full members of school leadership teams and directly responsible for raising student achievement and leading teachers. The year also includes intensive academic studies that further develop leadership skills. Once residents become principals, they continue to receive coaching as first-year principals, including support in diagnosing their school's needs and designing an action plan for improvement.

New Leaders principals serve in varied school settings. In 2009-10, 34 percent served in elementary schools, 13 percent in middle schools, and 20 percent in high schools. Other New Leaders principals serve in a range of grade-configured schools, with 23 percent in K-8 schools, 8 percent in middle/high schools, and 1 percent in K-12 schools. New Leaders principals serve in both charter and traditional district schools. Roughly 77 percent serve in traditional district schools, and 23 percent serve in public charter schools.

NYC Leadership Academy's Aspiring Principals Program

Since 2003, the NYC Leadership Academy's Aspiring Principals Program (APP) has recruited, prepared, and supported aspiring New York City public school leaders. APP is a standards-based, 14-month leadership development program that uses problem-based and action-learning methodologies to prepare participants to lead instructional improvement efforts in the city's high-need public schools—those marked by high poverty and low student achievement. Through its rigorous application process, APP selects a diverse and talented group of educators (including former assistant principals, teachers, coaches, and guidance counselors) deeply committed to closing the achievement gap. APP graduates commit to serve the New York City Department of Education (NYC DOE) for five years.

APP has three distinct phases: a six-week summer intensive that engages participants in a problem-based, action-learning curriculum that simulates the actual challenges of a New York City principalship; a 10-month, school-based residency under the mentorship of an experienced principal; and a planning summer that enables participants to transition successfully into school leadership positions. All participants are evaluated on a pass-fail basis and must meet rigorous performance standards to progress to each successive program phase and to graduate. The program is led by the APP faculty, which is comprised of former New York City principals and principal supervisors.

APP participants' salaries and benefits are paid by the NYC DOE while in the program. In addition, participants who have not yet earned their New York State administrative certification (SAS/SBL) will complete the necessary credits needed to qualify for SAS/SBL certification.

In 2009-10, APP principals represented 17 percent of New York City public school principals and currently serve more than 100,000 students. Since 2004, 21 percent of APP graduates have opened new, small New York City public schools.

RICE University's Education Entrepreneurship Program (REEP)

In 2008, Rice University, in Houston, TX, launched a series of programs for current and aspiring school leaders leveraging the capabilities of the Jones Graduate School of Business (JGSB). REEP offers both a degree track with a two-year MBA and a business certificate track. Both tracks focus on leadership development, business training, and education reform. REEP takes the approach that business training, coupled with an innovative education entrepreneurship summer institute, is the best way to prepare educators to become excellent school leaders.

REEP recruits applicants who have at least two (but three-plus is preferred) years of teaching experience and demonstrate excellence in instructional knowledge. REEP students are required to be employed in a Houston-area public school (district or charter), either as a teacher or administrator.

MBA Track: Students attend the Jones School's MBA for Professionals program for two years to build core business skills and a multi-industry network. During the summer, students attend the Education Entrepreneurship Summer Institute. The practicum after the summer includes a combination of skill development, coursework, and cohort-based work. All participants of the REEP program, if not currently certified, are required to take the Principal Certification Test as part of the program.

REEP offers tuition reimbursement to REEP MBA graduates who serve in a leadership position in Houston-area public schools for five years. The Houston Endowment has generously underwritten the majority of the MBA tuition and fees as well as the Summer Institute.

FOR MORE INFORMATION

Contact Andrea Hodge, Director, or visit: www.REEP.RICE.edu.

Business Certificate Track: For educators who already hold a master's degree and are looking for focused managerial and leadership training, REEP offers a 15-month business certificate program starting in the spring semester. It begins with monthly sessions throughout the spring, focused on business skill development. Participants then join the MBA students at the Education Entrepreneurship Institute. The practicum after the summer includes a combination of skill development, coursework, and cohort-based work. REEP students who do not possess the Principal Certification must take the TEXES exam prior to completing the course.

REEP Education Entrepreneurship Summer Institute: The REEP summer institute builds on the business skills foundation with an intense focus on what is possible in education. The focus is on critical thinking, problem-solving, and leadership responsibilities in schools.

School Leaders Network (SLN)

In 2006, School Leaders Network (SLN), based in Massachusetts, was formally established to address the leadership development needs of principals, to accelerate their learning in their efforts to increase student achievement, and to create a community of mentoring and support.

SLN's vision is that all school principals have the knowledge, skills, commitment, courage, and personal and professional attributes to guide, direct, and support that are needed to become leaders of high-performing schools. The mission of SLN is to expand educational opportunity for all students by transforming school leaders into empowered, highly effective principals who are capable of catalyzing change and driving increased student achievement at their schools. To achieve this mission, School Leaders Network provides the structure for public school principals to work together, to solve real problems, and to become innovative and inspired leaders who improve schools and student achievement, school-by-school, so that all students in under-resourced schools graduate with college-ready skills.

School leaders in 22 networks across the U.S. are provided with opportunities to identify, reflect on, and dialogue about critical leadership issues. Guided by a SLN-trained facilitator using the SLN research-based curriculum, networks engage in dynamic dialogues grappling with the complex challenges of student achievement, teacher capacity, and other critical leadership issues. Each network develops a professional community of practice and creates a space for participants to share and reflect on key issues and challenges in their respective schools. Principals share their knowledge, experience, and inspiration, empowering other members to translate problems into effective action. Leaders then engage one another in the process of identifying, analyzing, and solving a critical leadership issue that is co-constructed by the network. Leaders will take this model of inquiry back to their school community to solve the problems of student learning that are an impediment to student success.

More than a quarter of a million students across the country currently attend schools led by SLN-participating principals.

University of Illinois at Chicago's College of Education
Urban Education Leadership Program (UIC)

The Ed.D. in Urban Education Leadership develops principals and administrative educational leaders who transform low-performing urban schools, systems, and entire districts. The program includes at least three years of site-based coaching by former principals who have transformed urban schools and three years of field assessment aimed at producing candidates with proven ability as school change agents. The program has a strong emphasis on collection and analysis of data at the school level, which leads to a data-based capstone thesis that focuses on strategies of leadership practice.

UIC selects a diverse cohort from candidates who already hold a master's degree, who have demonstrated records of outstanding classroom instruction as well as instructional leadership as teachers or administrators, and who are clearly committed to transforming schools where the leadership need is most evident. Most members of each cohort come directly from teaching positions.

Candidates assume paid residencies in school leadership positions in Chicago Public Schools (CPS) early in the program, during which they receive coaching support. Following the residencies, nearly all candidates successfully obtain assistant principal or principal positions and receive coaching for a minimum of two more years.

UIC graduates are among the most highly sought-after administrators by local school councils in Chicago Public Schools. Of candidates who finish the academic-year residency in good standing, 96 percent have obtained administrative positions—most of them as principals—in Chicago schools. UIC-led schools outperform comparable CPS schools in measures of student performance and school climate and culture.

FOR MORE INFORMATION

Contact Steve Tozer, Professor and Founding Coordinator, or visit: education.uic.edu/uel-edd.

University of Virginia's Darden/Curry Partnership for Leaders in Education (PLE)

FOR MORE INFORMATION

Contact LeAnn M. Buntrock, Executive Director, or visit: www.darden.virginia.edu/web/ Darden-Curry-PLE.

In 2003, recognizing the need for such training and that effective leadership is as vital to success in education as it is in business, the University of Virginia's Darden School of Business and the Curry School of Education established a formal partnership—the Partnership for Leaders in Education (PLE).

The mission of the PLE is to strategically combine the most advanced thinking in business and education to meet the unique demands of managing and governing schools and school systems, proving that by engaging leadership at all levels and aligning those efforts, all students can learn at high levels.

The PLE offers a comprehensive two-year School Turnaround Specialist Program to school districts committed to turning around low-performing schools. The University of Virginia-School Turnaround Specialist Program (UVA-STSP) is the only school turnaround program in existence that utilizes a systemic approach to change by working with school, district, and, in some cases, state-level leadership teams to help them build the internal capacity necessary to support and sustain effective school turnarounds. The two-year program focuses on two components critical to successful and sustainable turnarounds: high-impact school leaders; and the district capacity/conditions necessary to initiate, support, and enhance transformational change. The program includes coursework, case studies, and discussions to share information and practical experience in proven business and education turnaround strategies. Content areas include assessment of personal leadership qualifications, skills to lead change, data analysis, decision making, setting targets, and creating action plans. School Turnaround Specialist Program participants also study business management strategies, organizational behavior and communication, and restructuring and renewal of troubled organizations.

Recognizing that there is no one formula for turning around a school, UVA-STSP works with education leaders to identify key issues and develop strategies based on their own school/district context. It does so by combining the type of executive education typically only received by top-level business leaders with ongoing support, resources, and tools for school and district teams. Consequently, the model is applicable in urban, suburban, and rural communities.

Results from the first four cohorts suggest that the specialist program is meeting its goal of raising student achievement in targeted schools. After two years in the UVA program, school performance increased by an average of 41 percent in reading and 44 percent in mathematics across all four cohorts. After three years, schools with UVA-trained leadership teams have more than doubled the number of students who scored proficient or better on state tests.

Endnotes

1. Leithwood, K., Louis, K.S., Anderson, S., and Wahlstrom, K. *How Leadership Influences Student Learning: Review of Research*, commissioned by The Wallace Foundation and produced jointly by the Center for Applied Research and Educational Improvement, the University of Minnesota, and Ontario Institute for Studies in Education, the University of Toronto, 2004, 5.

2. Leithwood, K., Louis, K. S., Anderson, S., and Wahlstrom, K. (2004) *Review of Research: How Leadership Influences Student Learning.* Wallace Foundation; and Marzano, R. J., Waters, T., and McNulty, B. (2005) *School Leadership That Works: From Research to Results.* Alexandria, VA: Association for Supervision and Curriculum Development.

3. Levine, Arthur (2006). Educating School Teachers. Washington, DC: The Education Schools Project.

4. Martorell, F., Heaton, P., Gates, S.M., and Hamilton, L.S. (2010). *Preliminary Findings from the New Leaders for New Schools Evaluation.* Santa Monica, CA: RAND, WR-739-NLNS.

5. Tuttle, C.C., Teh, B., Nichols-Barrer, I., Gill, B.P., and Gleason, P. *Student Characteristics and Achievement in 22 KIPP Middle Schools.* Mathematica Policy Research Inc., June 2010.

6. Corcoran, S.P., Schwartz, A.E., Weinstein, M. *The New York City Aspiring Principals Program: A School-Level Evaluation.* New York University's Institute for Education and Social Policy, August 2009.

7. The Interstate School Leaders Licensure Consortium (ISLLC) Standards align with the programs' Competency Frameworks, but most go beyond the ISLLC standards to crystalize those qualities that are most important in driving student achievement gains.

8. Public Impact is a national education policy and management consulting firm based in Chapel Hill, North Carolina. www.publicimpact.com.

9. In choosing an external tool, consider the validation of outcomes you seek and make sure the populations are reflective of your population.

10. Note: Gwinnett previously did a third residency during summer school but has since determined that the summer school experience was not as powerful as school-year experiences and, therefore, not an effective use of time and resources.

11. Developed by the New Teacher Center, Blended Coaching is a method of professional coaching in which the relationship is centered on addressing the needs of an individual in finding success in his/her work environment. Blended Coaching merges coaching, consulting, mentoring, and guided instruction. Coaches have expertise they can bring to the conversation, but they use this knowledge as a resource in collaborative planning moments. Blended Coaching allows the coach to focus on facilitation, inquiry, and curiosity, while still addressing gaps in knowledge, perspective, and experience.

12. Fuller, E., and Young, M.D. (2009) *Tenure and Retention of Newly Hired Principals in Texas.* University Council for Educational Administration, The University of Texas at Austin.

13. Tuttle, C.C., Teh, B., Nichols-Barrer, I., Gill, B.P., and Gleason, P. *Student Characteristics and Achievement in 22 KIPP Middle Schools.* Mathematica Policy Research Inc., June 2010.

14. Martorell, F., Heaton, P., Gates, S.M., and Hamilton, L.S. (2010). *Preliminary Findings from the New Leaders for New Schools Evaluation.* Santa Monica, CA: RAND, WR-739-NLNS.

15. Corcoran, S.P., Schwartz, A.E., and Weinstein, M. *The New York City Aspiring Principals Program: A School-Level Evaluation.* New York University's Institute for Education and Social Policy, August 2009.

Appendices

142 APPENDIX A: INTRODUCTION

143 Leadership Model

144 Logic Model Leadership Development

146 APPENDIX B: COMPETENCY FRAMEWORK

147 Leadership Framework and Competency Model

150 Leadership Performance Standards Matrix

157 APPENDIX C: BUILDING A CANDIDATE POOL

158 Recruitment Strategy

159 APPENDIX D: SELECTING CANDIDATES

160 Full Selection Criteria

162 Path to Principalship

164 Leadership Screening Fact Sheet

165 Protocol for the Classroom Instruction Video

166 Facilitated Group Interview

168 Interview Schedule

169 Selection Criteria Rubric Sample

170 Competency Scoring Sample

171 Sample Selection Matrix

172 APPENDIX E: TRAINING AND DEVELOPING FELLOWS

173 Residency Compact

176 Individual Learning Plan Summary Document

177 Summer Intensive Themes

178 Summer Intensive Sample Days

182 Foundational Year Scope & Sequence

192 Residency Summary

193 Recommendations on Identifying
and Choosing Coaches

194 APPENDIX F: SUPPORTING PRINCIPALS

195 Mentor Program Fact Sheet

196 Summer Leadership Conference

197 Sample Network Meeting Plan

199 Just-in-Time Training Fact Sheet

APPENDIX A

Introduction

Leadership Model

SOURCE: Gwinnett County Public Schools Quality-Plus Leader Academy

Situation: Principals are a major driver of school improvement and teacher quality, and second only to teachers in their impact on student achievement. Gwinnett County Public Schools Quality-Plus Leader Academy (QPLA) provides the leadership development model, coupled with coherent and successful programs, to drive improvement in seven major elements that ultimately lead to improvement in student achievement. These elements include pipeline development, recruitment, selection, training, placement, on-going support, and evaluation and assessment.

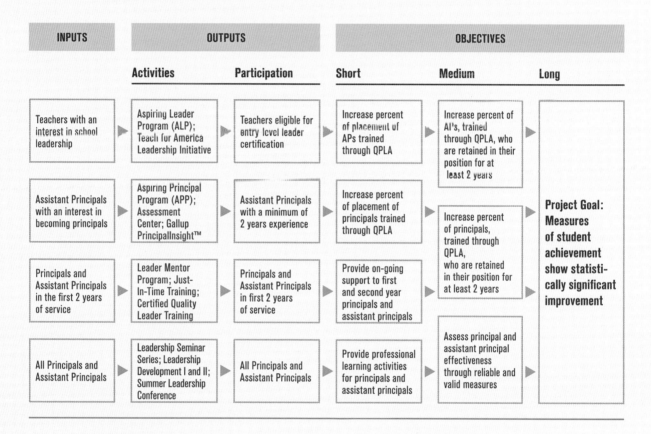

Assumptions

Pre-service and in-service school leaders who receive appropriate training and support will have a positive impact on student achievement when compared to others without comparable training and support.

External Factors

Inadequate preparation and support of school leaders through traditional preparation programs contribute to less than desired long range goals.

Evaluation

Individual activities will be evaluated for client satisfaction and alignment with stated objectives. Overall, the program will use internal evaluation and external or third-party evaluation to assess progress on objectives.

Logic Model Leadership Development

SOURCE: Gwinnett County Public Schools Quality-Plus Leader Academy

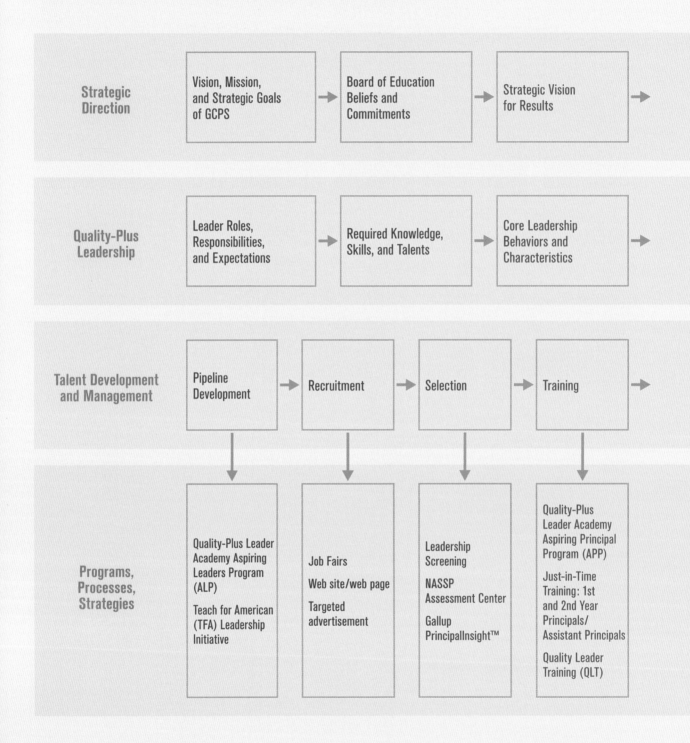

Strategic Direction

Vision, Mission, and Strategic Goals of GCPS → Board of Education Beliefs and Commitments → Strategic Vision for Results →

Quality-Plus Leadership

Leader Roles, Responsibilities, and Expectations → Required Knowledge, Skills, and Talents → Core Leadership Behaviors and Characteristics →

Talent Development and Management

Pipeline Development → Recruitment → Selection → Training →

Programs, Processes, Strategies

Quality-Plus Leader Academy Aspiring Leaders Program (ALP)

Teach for American (TFA) Leadership Initiative

Job Fairs

Web site/web page

Targeted advertisement

Leadership Screening

NASSP Assessment Center

Gallup PrincipalInsight™

Quality-Plus Leader Academy Aspiring Principal Program (APP)

Just-in-Time Training: 1st and 2nd Year Principals/ Assistant Principals

Quality Leader Training (QLT)

144

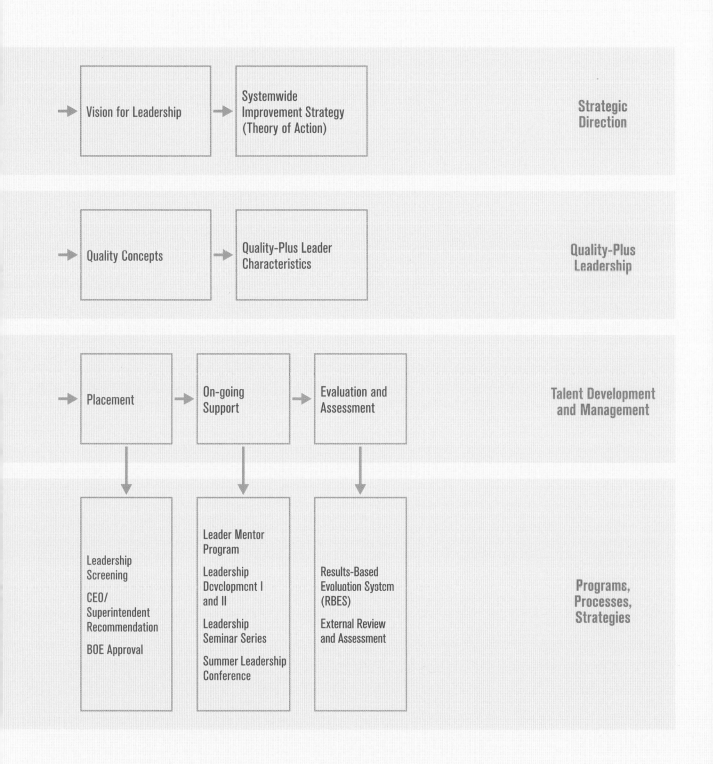

Vision for Leadership → Systemwide Improvement Strategy (Theory of Action) — Strategic Direction

Quality Concepts → Quality-Plus Leader Characteristics — Quality-Plus Leadership

Placement → On-going Support → Evaluation and Assessment — Talent Development and Management

Placement: Leadership Screening; CEO/Superintendent Recommendation; BOE Approval

On-going Support: Leader Mentor Program; Leadership Development I and II; Leadership Seminar Series; Summer Leadership Conference

Evaluation and Assessment: Results-Based Evaluation System (RBES); External Review and Assessment

— Programs, Processes, Strategies

APPENDIX B

Competency Framework

Leadership Framework and Competency Model
SOURCE: **KIPP School Leadership Program**

Introduction

The KIPP Leadership Framework and Competency Model describes the competencies and behaviors considered most important to the performance of KIPP Executive Directors, Principals, Vice Principals/Deans and Grade Level Chairs/other teacher leaders, leaders in our regional shared services teams and KIPP Foundation staff.

Our leadership framework is the high-level category architecture that assists in organizing our competencies and showing how those competencies relate to one another. A competency can be defined as "a cluster of related knowledge, skills and attitudes that affects a major part of one's job (a role or responsibility), that correlates with performance on the job, that can be measured against well-accepted standards, and that can be improved via training and development" (Parry, 1996, p.50).

Every competency in this model includes key behaviors that make up the competency. The key behaviors within each competency describe the actions a leader takes that demonstrate proficiency in that competency.

This model lays the foundation for several associated tools that will enable us to more effectively select, develop, evaluate, retain, and promote leadership at KIPP. Leadership development tools associated with this model include evaluation tools, goal-setting tools, 360 feedback tools, proficiency and leadership development roadmaps, realistic job preview tools, interview protocols, and selection rubrics.

Description of the Framework and Competency Model

Effective KIPP leaders Drive Results, Build Relationships, and Manage People. They do so in order to Prove the Possible for our students. As such, we've organized our core framework and competencies into these four categories. Every individual also has critical role-specific competencies that may vary by role across regions and as you cross from school leadership into regional leadership. Essential competencies such as Instructional Leadership and Operations Management fit in this category. The Role-specific Competencies category rings the core competencies because these competencies often make up a very visible part of an individual's role and because they often rely upon many of the underlying core competencies.

The Prove the Possible category and Student Focus competency are at the middle of our model, helping to always center the efforts of our leaders with a constant focus on what's best for students. The Drive Results category includes core competencies that are directly associated with the individual's ability to produce exceptional outcomes and their ability to model and support others in producing exceptional outcomes. The Build Relationships category includes competencies that enable our leaders to work effectively with others. The Manage People category includes competencies that all leaders must demonstrate to ensure that staff and team performance are excellent. Role-specific Competencies include specialized knowledge and skills that are extremely important and highly visible to some, but not all leadership roles at KIPP. For example KIPP Executive Directors and Principals must demonstrate operational skills and knowledge that are not required for KIPP Grade Level Chairs. This category allows flexibility for regional organizations to apply this model to Shared Services Team members whose roles may also require essential domain expertise.

SELECTION RUBRIC
Based on the KIPP School Leadership Program Framework and Competency Model

Drive Results
Achievement Orientation
Continuous Learning
Critical Thinking and Problem-solving
Decision Making
Planning and Execution

Build Relationships
Stakeholder Management
Communication
Impact and Influence
Self-awareness
Cultural Competence

Manage People
Direction Setting
Team Leadership
Performance Management
Talent Development

Background and Research Base

The KIPP Leadership Competency Model is both empirically derived and heavily research-based. To create this model we relied partly upon the practical experience of high performing KIPP leaders at all levels and those at KIPP Foundation who work with those leaders. Through both discussions and focus groups, our leaders offered perspective on what competencies are most important to their effectiveness. Focus groups validated this model by providing role-specific examples of every key behavior in the model. We also relied significantly upon research in the organizational, business, and education domains that indicated which competencies and behaviors are most tied to effective leadership, management and student achievement. This research helped us to both prioritize competencies and structure the key behaviors that demonstrate proficiency in those competencies.

Note: This example of one key area (Drive Results) is provided for illustration—each area is developed out in detail like this for the complete KIPP Competency Framework model.

DRIVE RESULTS: Achievement Orientation
Key Behaviors: An Effective KIPP Leader...

▶ CHALLENGING GOALS. Demonstrates high expectations by setting challenging goals for him or herself and others.

▶ INITIATIVE. Takes initiative, going above and beyond typical expectations and making necessary sacrifices to achieve exceptional results.

▶ FOLLOW THROUGH. Follows through on commitments and promises with an appropriate sense of urgency.

▶ RESILIENCE. Demonstrates tenacity, persevering through significant challenges to reach goals. Supports perseverance in others.

▶ FLEXIBILITY. Demonstrates flexibility when plans or situations change unexpectedly. Effectively adjusts plans to achieve intended outcomes.

▶ FOCUS ON RESULTS. Focuses upon results and how they are achieved. Does not confuse effort with results.

DRIVE RESULTS: Continuous Learning
Key Behaviors: An Effective KIPP Leader...

▶ LEARNING. Takes responsibility for behavior, mistakes, and results, learns from successes and failures, and teaches others to do the same.

▶ RISK TAKING. Takes calculated risks and teaches others to do the same.

▶ DATA-BASED IMPROVEMENTS. Uses data to accurately assess areas for improvement and teaches others to do the same.

▶ RESEARCH. Uses research to inform practices.

▶ IMPROVEMENT. Continuously and humbly seeks opportunities for personal and organizational improvement. Proactively solicits and willingly accepts assistance.

▶ INNOVATION. Values and encourages creative and innovative ideas.

▶ SHARING. Promotes and contributes to a culture of sharing effective practices within the organization and across the KIPP network.

DRIVE RESULTS: Critical Thinking and Problem Solving
Key Behaviors: An Effective KIPP Leader...

▶ GATHERING INFORMATION. Gathers information from multiple relevant sources and stakeholders when problem-solving.

▶ SORTING OUT COMPLEXITY. Identifies useful relationships among complex data from unrelated areas.

▶ ANTICIPATING PROBLEMS. Anticipates and identifies problems in a timely manner.

▶ BREAKING DOWN INFORMATION. Breaks complex information and problems into parts.

▶ ANALYSIS. Analyzes, reflects upon, synthesizes, and contextualizes information.

▶ WEIGHING OPTIONS. Weighs pros and cons of multiple options to solve complex problems.

DRIVE RESULTS: Decision-Making
Key Behaviors: An Effective KIPP Leader...

▶ PROCESSES. Establishes decision-making processes, communicating about how decisions will be made and who has input, and ensuring that decisions are made by individuals best suited to make them.

▶ CONSEQUENCES. Considers both the longer-term and unintended consequences of potential decisions.

▶ SENSE OF URGENCY. Makes timely decisions, using intuition as well as data in the face of ambiguity.

▶ COMMUNICATING. Timely conveys decisions to relevant stakeholders and takes follow-up actions to support decisions.

▶ DIFFICULT CHOICES. Willingly makes and stands by controversial decisions that benefit the organization. Shares understanding of the rationale for decisions, particularly when consensus cannot be reached.

DRIVING RESULTS: Planning and Execution
Key Behaviors: An Effective KIPP Leader...

▶ BACKWARD PLANNING. Methodically backward plans to achieve short-and long-term goals.

▶ RESOURCES. Accurately scopes and secures resources needed to accomplish projects.

▶ PRIORITIZING. Manages time and resources effectively, prioritizing efforts according to organizational goals.

▶ ACCOUNTABILITY. Regularly compares actual progress to planned milestones and adjusts plans accordingly, holding him or herself and others accountable for achieving intended outcomes.

▶ CONTINGENCY PLANS. Proactively develops contingency plans in advance of potential or unforeseen circumstances.

Leadership Performance Standards Matrix

SOURCE: **NYC Leadership Academy**

Leadership Dimension	Meeting the Standard	Progressing toward the Standard	Not meeting the Standard
1.0 Personal Behavior			
1.1 Reflects an appropriate response to situations	Leader considers the consequence of his/her actions, anticipates possible responses or reactions, and accurately adjusts behavior accordingly. Leader understands and manages emotions and is aware of their impact.	Leader usually considers the consequence of his/her actions. Leader adjusts behavior accordingly. Although aware of impact on others, leader is unable to always manage emotions. It is evident that leader is continually working toward managing emotions.	Leader often responds and reacts emotionally. Leader seldom considers the unintended consequences of his/her actions.
1.2 Consistent with expressed belief system and reflect personal integrity	Leader's behavior reflects core values at all times. Leader's actions are transparent and there are no surprises.	Leader's core values guide almost all behaviors. Leader's actions are usually transparent and there are few surprises.	Leader's behaviors are not driven by values that are recognizable. Leader's actions are not transparent with expressed belief system and surprise others.
1.3 Complies with legal and ethical requirements in relationships with employees and students	Leader understands the intent of the law and uses it to ensure the rights of employees and students are fully protected.	Leader is sufficiently familiar with the intent of the law to ensure compliance in protecting the rights of employees and students.	Leader violates—even just one time—the legal and policy requirements for the relationship between leaders and employees and students.
1.4 Values different points of view within the organization	Leader actively seeks and makes use of diverse and controversial views. Leader welcomes and appreciates diversity in demonstrable ways.	Leader usually or when approached makes use of diverse and controversial views. Leader is continually working towards valuing diversity.	Leader avoids diverse and controversial views. Leader suppresses other points of view and discourages disagreement or divergent thinking.
1.5 Reflects appropriate professional demeanor	Leader expresses and behaves in a way that is respectful of the norms, values, and culture of the organization.	Leader understands the norms, values, and culture of the organization but is not always consistent in behaving that way.	Leader's actions and behavior does not consider the norms, values, and culture of the organization.
2.0 Resilience			
2.1 Reacts constructively to disappointment, admits error, and learns from mistakes and setbacks	Leader quickly transitions from emotional to strategic responses to mistakes and setbacks.	Leader generally successful in transitioning from emotional to strategic responses to mistakes and setbacks.	Leader's emotional responses to disappointment, mistakes and setbacks inhibit transition to strategic responses.
2.2 Maintains mental focus and energy in the face of difficult situations	Leader is able to focus on solutions and integrate conflicting/competing directives to effectively solve problems. Leader demonstrates capacity to analyze, synthesize, and promote coherence.	Leader is clearly focused on problem solving. Leader is generally successful at analyzing, synthesizing, and promoting coherence.	Leader is unable to focus on solutions. Leader's decisions are implemented without awareness of the need for integration.

A NEW APPROACH TO PRINCIPAL PREPARATION

Leadership Dimension	Meeting the Standard	Progressing toward the Standard	Not meeting the Standard
2.3 Handles disagreement and dissent constructively	Leader transforms disagreement and dissent into opportunities.	Leader is generally successful in using disagreement and dissent to create opportunities.	Leader is not successful in using disagreement and dissent to create opportunities.
2.4 Uses formal and informal feedback to improve performance	Leader seeks out feedback. Leader's 360° feedback results in action plan aligned to leader's strategic priorities.	Leader accepts feedback when approached. Leader's 360° feedback is occasionally included in leader's strategic priorities.	Leader avoids or does not value feedback. Leader's 360° feedback is not evident in the leader's priorities.
2.5 Is able to deal with ambiguities	Leader is able to take the information available and make decisions as appropriate.	Leader is hesitant to make decisions without seeking additional facts regardless of circumstances.	Leader is unable to take action without absolute clarity about all factors.

3.0 Communication

Leadership Dimension	Meeting the Standard	Progressing toward the Standard	Not meeting the Standard
3.1 Two-way communication with students	Leader interacts with student body on a consistent basis. Leader both encourages and models to staff members to purposefully solicit student ideas regarding successful classroom approaches to teaching and learning.	Leader interacts with student body. Leader is trying to encourage and model to staff members to purposefully solicit student ideas regarding successful classroom approaches to teaching and learning.	Leader is not familiar with student body. Leader does not encourage nor model to staff to solicit ideas from students.
3.2 Two-way communication with faculty and staff	Leader knows all staff members and publicly acknowledges individual contributions. Leader matches media with message. Leader always focuses staff meetings on instructional issues.	Leader knows all staff members and attempts to publicly acknowledge individual contributions. Leader generally matches media with message. Leader usually focuses staff meetings on instructional issues.	Leader knows some staff members. Leader uses limited media and does not appear able to match the media with the message. Public address system and other electronic devices often interrupt the educational process. Leader usually uses staff meetings for announcements.
3.3 Two-way communication with parents and community	Leader establishes interactions with parents and community members. Leader develops clear processes for gathering and transmitting information from and to parents.	Leader is working on developing interactions with parents and community members. Leader periodically gathers information from and sends information to parents.	Leader reserves interactions with parents and community members for crisis situations. Leader lacks processes or interest in communicating with parents.
3.4 Communication is clear and appropriate for the audience	Leader's communication is clear and appropriate for the audience. Leader understands cultural patterns and adjusts his/her communication style accordingly. Leader consistently listens and checks for mutual understanding. Leader's presentations are organized, logical, and include analysis of information; the style is engaging and dynamic. Leader provides clear, specific responses to audience questions.	Leader's communication is planned to meet the needs of the audience and the occasion. Leader is working to understand cultural patterns and adjust his/her communication style accordingly. Leader generally checks for mutual understanding. Leader's presentations are usually organized and logical; the style is generally engaging and dynamic. Leader attempts to provide clear, specific responses to audience questions.	Leader uses the same communication style regardless of the context or audience. Leader does not consider cultural patterns in communication. Leader does not listen or check for understanding. Leader's presentations are loose and disorganized; style is not engaging. Leader does not respond clearly to audience or avoids questions from audience.

Leadership Dimension	Meeting the Standard	Progressing toward the Standard	Not meeting the Standard
3.5 Communication with the public	Leader communicates with individuals consistently in attention, time, and respect given. Leader demonstrates awareness of the public and political nature of his/her position and applies explicit process for engaging the public in controversial issues.	Leader attempts to communicate with public/individuals consistently in attention, time, and respect given. Leader demonstrates awareness of the public and political nature of his/her position and is able to engage the public in controversial issues.	Leader does not give the same attention, time, and respect to individuals. Leader avoids public dialogue, or appoints someone else to be the spokesperson and does not demonstrate the ability to engage the public in controversial issues.
3.6 Communication reflects careful analysis and the ability to listen	Leader attends and responds to subtle nonverbal cues in others. Leader deals with difficult issues honestly and directly, uses low-inference data and provides examples. Leader actively pursues disconfirming evidence for conclusions drawn.	Leader responds to common nonverbal cues in others. Leader deals with difficult issues promptly, uses low-inference data and provides examples. Leader often pursues disconfirming evidence for conclusions drawn.	Leader avoids difficult issues. Leader does not appear to communicate openly, uses high-inference, and is often accused of holding back information from others.
4.0 Focus on Student Performance			
4.1 Plans and sets goals for student performance	Leader sets goals that are within the zone of proximal development for students, teachers, and the organization.	Leader is generally successful at setting goals that are within zone of proximal development for students, teachers, and the organization.	Leader has no understanding of or does not employ the zone of proximal development and its role in order to establish goals.
4.2 Ensures continual improvement for students, teachers, and the organization	Leader possesses working knowledge of current curricular initiatives, approaches to content and differentiated instructional design. Leader understands and can articulate effective instructional strategies. Leader implements these strategies and evaluates their effectiveness.	Leader is working towards understanding current curricular initiatives, approaches to content and differentiated instructional design. Leader understands and can generally articulate effective instructional strategies. Leader occasionally implements these strategies and evaluates their effectiveness.	Leader does not understand the need for continual improvement.
4.3 Demonstrates understanding of the relationship between assessment, standards, and curriculum	Leader facilitates the analysis and alignment of assessment tools and the curriculum. Leader organizes around instructional priorities to address standards that will leverage student learning.	Leader understands the analysis and alignment of assessment tools and the curriculum. Leader is generally successful at organizing around instructional priorities to address standards that will leverage student learning.	Leader does not understand nor articulates the relationship between assessment, standards, and curriculum.
4.4 Is transparent in reporting student achievement results	Leader gathers and uses multiple indicators of student success that reveal patterns, trends, and insights. Leader creates systems to make data accessible and understood by students, parents, and teachers.	Leader gathers multiple indicators of student success. Leader is in the process of creating systems to make student achievement data accessible and understood by students, parents, and teachers.	Leader uses single data points. Leader makes student achievement results available but is not concerned with checking for understanding or the accessibility of such information.
4.5 Uses student performance data to make instructional leadership decisions	Leader uses student performance data for instructional decision making. Leader provides structure for looking at student work to identify instructional next steps for teachers and students.	Leader is creating the system to use student performance data for instructional decision making. Leader is creating the structure for looking at student work to identify instructional next steps for teachers and students.	Leader makes instructional decisions without the use of student performance data. Leader does not understand the need to review student work for instructional next steps.

A NEW APPROACH TO PRINCIPAL PREPARATION

Leadership Dimension	Meeting the Standard	Progressing toward the Standard	Not meeting the Standard
4.6 Implements a systemic approach for struggling learners and special populations and critically reviews all approaches for effectiveness	Leader monitors intervention strategies for effectiveness and adjusts them to accelerate learning. Leader infuses specialized knowledge and skills into general practice.	Leader occasionally monitors intervention strategies for effectiveness and adjusts them to accelerate learning. Leader is in the process of infusing specialized knowledge and skills into general practice.	Leader does not monitor intervention strategies for effectiveness. Leader does not infuse the expertise of special education providers into general practice.
4.7 Continually reads and interprets the environment to identify patterns in student performance indicators	Leader uses a multi-dimensional environmental analysis of student performance indicators. Diagnosis is ongoing.	Leader is learning about multidimensional environmental analysis of student performance indicators. Diagnosis is ongoing.	Leader relies on one-dimensional factors to explain student performance.

5.0 Situational Problem-Solving

Leadership Dimension	Meeting the Standard	Progressing toward the Standard	Not meeting the Standard
5.1 Uses evidence as basis for decisionmaking	Leader interprets and analyzes multiple sources of state, district and classroom level student performance data to make decisions.	Leader generally interprets and analyzes one or more forms of state, district, and classroom level student performance data to make decisions.	Leader makes decisions without the use of student performance data.
5.2 Clearly identifies decision-making structure	Leader builds professional relationships, empowers and engages staff in decision-making. Leader is able to make decisions alone when required.	Leader generally builds professional relationships, engages staff in decision-making. Leader makes decisions alone only when required.	Leader does not build professional relationships nor engage staff in decision-making. Leader is unable to make decisions alone.
5.3 Links decisions to strategic priorities	Leader links decisions to goals, objectives, and priorities. Leader consistently evaluates decisions for effectiveness in furthering strategic instructional priorities. Leader consistently raises decisions that are not working.	While goals and priorities are clear, leader does not consistently link them to decisions. Leader usually evaluates decisions for effectiveness in furthering instructional priorities. Leader can discuss decisions that are not working.	Leader is unaware of or disconnected from the goals, objectives, and priorities. Leader does not evaluate decisions. Leader is unable to identify ineffective decisions and when confronted sticks to old decisions.
5.4 Exercises professional judgment	Leader reflects on and is mindful of rules, procedures, and regulations. As a result of this process, leader's decisions reflect the values and beliefs of the organization.	Leader reflects on and is mindful of rules, procedures, and regulations. Despite the reflection, leader's decisions do not align with values or beliefs of the organization.	Leader makes decisions without consideration of appropriate rules, procedures, and regulations.

6.0 Learning

Leadership Dimension	Meeting the Standard	Progressing toward the Standard	Not meeting the Standard
6.1 Applies research trends in education and leadership	Leader consistently uses research to inform instructional and organizational decisions. Leader creates a system for communicating this knowledge via reading, learning, and reflecting with the staff.	Leader demonstrates occasional use of research to inform instructional and organizational decisions. Leader is in the process of creating a system for communicating this knowledge via reading, learning and reflecting with the staff.	Leader does not use research to inform instructional or organizational decisions.

Leadership Dimension	Meeting the Standard	Progressing toward the Standard	Not meeting the Standard
6.2 Understands the role of a learner	Leader is able to identify and take ownership of professional and leadership development needs. Leader understands that the best ideas emerge and are acted upon regardless of the source. Leader values mistakes in the service of learning and moves from the known to the unknown. Leader uses feedback and self-reflection to enhance own learning.	Leader is able to identify and/or take ownership of professional and leadership development needs when prompted. Leader is working towards understanding that the best ideas emerge and are acted upon regardless of the source. Leader occasionally values mistakes in the service of learning and generally moves from the known to the unknown. Leader uses feedback and self-reflection to enhance learning inconsistently.	Leader is unable to identify learning needs. Leader evaluates ideas based on the source. Leader believes his/her own ideas are most worthy. Leader does not value mistakes. Leader resists feedback and does not value self-reflection in the service of learning.
6.3 Understands and utilizes theories of learning and change	Leader uses knowledge of theories of learning and change to respond strategically to immediate and long term challenges. Leader understands that learning drives the system and every action is in the service of learning.	Leader uses knowledge of theories of learning and change to respond to challenges. Leader understands that learning drives the system and most actions are in the service of learning.	Leader does not understand the change process. Leader may believe in learning but does not structure the environment in the service of learning.
6.4 Develops plan for professional growth	Leader actively pursues personal professional development that is directly linked to organizational needs.	Leader engages in personal professional development.	Leader does not understand the need for continuous learning.
7.0 Accountability for Professional Practice			
7.1 Continually reads and interprets the environment of professional practice in order to identify patterns, needs for development, and leverage points for actions	Leader organizes a system for identified learning based on observed patterns and feedback. Leader provides opportunities and resources for learning to take place. Leader can lead multi-dimensional environmental analysis for adults and the organization.	Leader identifies learning needs based on observed patterns. Leader is working to provide opportunities and resources for learning to take place. Leader is learning about multidimensional environmental analysis for adults and the organization.	Leader provides professional development that is typically "one size fits all" and there is little or no evidence of recognition of individual faculty needs. Leader relies on one-dimensional factors to explain the environment of professional practice.
7.2 Employs strategies to maximize learning opportunities	Leader uses time and provides focus, coherence, and synthesis to maximize learning opportunities.	Leader is learning to use time, provide focus and provides coherence to maximize learning opportunities.	Leader does not see the value in using time and providing learning opportunities to the staff.
7.3 Matches learning to the learner	Leader employs strategies to differentiate learning opportunities for adult learners. Leader is aware of the various adult learning styles and supports the use of a variety of approaches and strategies to maximize learning.	Leader employs some strategies to differentiate learning opportunities for adult learners. Leader is developing a familiarity with the various adult learning styles and is trying to support the use of a variety of approaches and strategies to maximize learning.	Leader does not understand the importance of differentiating learning opportunities for adult learners.
7.4 Employs feedback mechanisms for adult learners	Leader puts a variety of structures in place (macro and micro) for the community to engage in feedback that is focused on improving performance.	Leader provides some opportunity for the community to engage in feedback that is usually focused on improving performance.	Leader allows for feedback to be formulaic, sporadic, and unspecific.

A NEW APPROACH TO PRINCIPAL PREPARATION

Leadership Dimension	Meeting the Standard	Progressing toward the Standard	Not meeting the Standard
8.0 Supervision of Instructional and Non-instructional staff			
8.1 Is able to make decisions and deal with consequences	Leader exhibits willingness to make tough decisions and deal with the difficult circumstances. Leader employs strategies for implementing tough decisions and considers possible consequences and opportunities following the decision.	Leader exhibits willingness to make some tough decisions and deal with the difficult circumstances. Leader occasionally tailors strategies for implementing tough decisions to the needs of individuals.	Leader is not willing to make tough decisions and deal with the difficult circumstances. Leader makes decisions in haste, anger, or out of emotion.
8.2 Values reflective practice	Leader creates environment in which everyone can question own assumptions in light of evidence and while maintaining non-negotiables. Leader creates systems that encourage reflective practice.	Leader creates environment in which some staff are comfortable questioning own assumptions in light of evidence and while maintaining non-negotiables. Leader creates systems that encourage reflective practice.	The environment does not encourage others to question their assumptions. The leader's actions do not support understanding of the need for reflective practice. Leader does not engage in reflective practice.
8.3 Sets a system for clear expectations	Leader has established performance and behavior expectations for adults and students that are consistent with best practice, high professional standards, and educational research. Leader frequently checks for understanding.	Leader has established performance and behavior expectations for adults and students that are consistent with regulatory requirements. Leader is developing ways to check for understanding.	Leader is not clear about performance and behavior expectations for students or staff. Leader's own behavior is inconsistent with expectations for others.
8.4 Cultivates a system of evaluation	Leader creates systems to provide a variety of ways to meet with teachers, share expectations, provide feedback and clearly check for understanding. Leader organizes environment to hold staff accountable. Leader uses observation information systematically to identify patterns needing improvement. Leader actively coaches instructional staff for improvement in classroom practice.	Leader uses a variety of ways to meet with teachers, share expectations, provide feedback, and clearly check for understanding. Leader is working towards organizing the environment to hold staff accountable. Leader uses observation information to identify patterns needing improvement. Leader occasionally coaches instructional staff for improvement in classroom practice.	Leader only uses "formal observations" to provide information to teachers. Leader's behavior indicates a lack of understanding of the value of coaching the staff to improve. Leader has not organized for staff accountability. Leader is inconsistent about using observation information for improvement. Leader does not coach the staff to improve classroom practice.
9.0 Leadership Development			
9.1 Develops leadership in others	Leader provides formal and informal leadership opportunities for others and encourages them to exercise appropriate authority in those areas for which they are held accountable.	Leader provides some formal and informal leadership opportunities for others and lets them occasionally exercise authority in areas for which they are held accountable.	Leader reserves almost all decisionmaking authority, confuses delegating tasks with leadership development and leaves others unable to exercise independent judgment.
9.2 Identifies and nurtures potential future leaders	Leader routinely identifies and provides opportunities to mentor, guide, and develop emerging leaders. Leader models the behavior that he/she expects and wants to see in others.	Leader tries to identify and makes effort to provide occasional opportunities to mentor, guide, and develop emerging leaders. Leader occasionally models the behavior that he/she expects and wants to see in others.	Leader appears to be indifferent to the need for leadership development in others.

Leadership Performance Standards Matrix continued

Leadership Dimension	Meeting the Standard	Progressing toward the Standard	Not meeting the Standard
10.0 Climate and Culture			
10.1 Motivates and encourages others to achieve strategic goals	Leader models, encourages, and reinforces efficacy in individuals to produce results and persevere even when internal and external difficulties interfere with the achievement of strategic goals. Leader generates a sense of urgency by aligning the energy of others in pursuit of its strategic priorities.	Leader encourages and attempts to reinforce efficacy In individuals to produce results. Leader attempts to generate a sense of urgency by aligning the energy of others in pursuit of its strategic priorities.	Leader has not been able to model efficacy or motivate the staff. Leader is personally discouraged.
10.2 Appreciates rituals and routines as enablers of vision	Leader develops consistent patterns of rituals and routines and understands how they enable the leader's vision and strategic priorities. Leader understands and honors the organization's existing culture of rituals and routines.	Leader's rituals and routines can be observed and often support strategic priorities. Leader is developing the understanding of organization's existing culture of rituals and routines.	Leader's rituals and routines are not evident or existing rituals and routines are implemented without awareness of their potential for enabling vision. Leader does not understand or disregards organizational climate and culture.
10.3 Clearly articulates non-negotiables	Leader has clearly established boundaries for behaviors that are considered fixed and immovable.	Leader has established boundaries for many behaviors that are considered fixed and immovable.	Leader has not established boundaries for behavior.
11.0 Time/Task/Project Management			
11.1 Consistently manages time in relationship to priorities	Leader clearly establishes daily priorities and objectives. Leader distinguishes between interruptions that are (a) important, (b) urgent, or (c) represent distractions. Leader aligns organizational priorities and daily activities. Leader removes/delegates nonessential tasks. Leader engages in calendar analysis to assess use of time.	Leader establishes daily priorities and objectives. Leader is usually successful at distinguishing between interruptions that are (a) important, (b) urgent, or (c) represent distractions. Leader generally aligns organizational priorities and daily activities. Leader occasionally removes/delegates non-essential tasks. Leader is learning to engage in calendar analysis to assess use of time.	Leader's daily objectives appear haphazard and not prioritized. Leader is always involved with urgent interruptions, even if they are unimportant. Leader does not align organizational priorities and daily activities. Leader sees no need to assess his/her daily use of time since he/she has been busy all day.
11.2 Sets clear objectives and coherent plans for complex projects	Leader plans projects using clear and written lists of milestones, deadlines, and persons responsible.	Leader is becoming successful at planning projects using clear and written lists of milestones, deadlines, and persons responsible.	Leader's project and team management is haphazard or nonexistent. There is little or no evidence of lists of milestones and deadlines.
11.3 Manages resources to complete projects	Leader is strategic in selection of resources, meeting deadlines, frequent communication and supporting if necessary.	Leader usually manages the selection of resources, meeting deadlines, frequent communication and supporting if necessary.	Leader does not manage nor is strategic in selection of resources, meeting deadlines, frequent communication and supporting if necessary.
12.0 Technology			
12.1 Demonstrates use of technology to improve communication, teaching, and learning	Leader uses technology personally in a competent manner and links technology initiatives of the organization to specific teaching and learning objectives.	Leader is personally proficient in technology and advocates for the use of instructional technology.	Leader does not display personal competence in technology applications and does not link the installation of technology to specific teaching and learning objectives.

A NEW APPROACH TO PRINCIPAL PREPARATION

APPENDIX C

Building a Candidate Pool

Recruitment Strategy

SOURCE: **New Leaders for New Schools**

Annual Goal	Key Strategies	Key Tactics
Successfully recruit 150 high-quality candidates to apply to ensure matriculate 12–15 diverse, high quality candidates into program. 10–12 for district, 4–5 for charters	Identify high potential candidates	Build and leverage a strong nominator network ▸ Engage regional outstanding public district and charter school principals who have improved their schools. ID through word-of-mouth, improved student outcomes over their tenure, awards they have won, district leadership or charter networks ▸ Engage PD organizations, nonprofits, Asst. Superintendents, trainers or others who have direct contact with teachers, teacher leaders, and APs either in school buildings or through other programs where they see their skills ▸ Engage nonprofits and special programs (e.g. NASA teacher corps, Carnegie Science Teachers) to learn about their teacher pool ▸ Review teacher, teacher leaders and AP award winners over past 5 years ▸ Work with Teach For America and The New Teacher Project to review all their alumni in the region who might be ready this year, and next 2 ▸ Track teachers with high student achievement gains ▸ Track down names of teacher leaders, Dept. Chairs, instructional leaders–who have helped improve their schools. Get roster from districts and charters. Cross reference against school improvement data.
	Target high-potential candidates	Target each high potential candidate with appropriate communication, information, and support from staff and New Leaders throughout the process Send out nomination letters/emails and make calls to each, inviting them to attend an info session. Offer Targeted Follow Up Options: ▸ Connect them with program graduates ▸ Take them on planned school visit to talk with program graduate principal about new model of principal leadership ▸ Have them speak to Executive Director or other senior program leader ▸ Have a district or charter leader contact them Hold special info sessions with Teach For America, The New Teacher Project and other organizations with high-performing teachers and teacher leaders Track in database what is learned about candidates–their likelihood of applying, their interests, their questions. Follow up regularly, especially with strong candidates who appear persuadable or seem really interested. Identify strong prospects for next few years–who may not yet be ready this year–and provide feedback that allows them to develop to meet selection criteria.
	Spread the word broadly	Solicit earned media, including a Back to School article in the newspaper, highlight successful principals
		Utilize and include external partners in the selection process (especially Finalist Days)–so they become familiar with program and profile of right fit candidate to become future nominators
		Develop advertising fliers to post at schools, other appropriate venues, mail to all principals and request they post at schools
		Hold Information Sessions
		Email principals, charter leaders about opportunity for their teams.
		Blast email letter about opportunity to all PD and training organizations, education nonprofits, community leaders, teacher lists, charter lists, district leaders.
Kick off recruiting after Labor Day to have 30% applicants for December and 70% March deadlines	Update Database over summer Refine recruiting plan	Clean up database and collect information on candidates. Tag with tiering system with high-potential to apply and high-potential to be selected. Review what sources had the highest yield in selection process. Develop a recruitment calendar, including information sessions and other events, that reflects prospects' needs and supports high potential candidates throughout the process.

APPENDIX D

Selecting Candidates

Full Selection Criteria

SOURCE: **New Leaders for New Schools**

The following Selection Criteria summarize the characteristics shared by every New Leaders principal and are the basis for all admissions decisions.

Beliefs and Orientation

Belief and Urgency that All Students will Excel Academically

▷ Demonstrate the belief that every student, regardless of background, can excel academically
▷ Demonstrate a sense of urgency to achieve dramatic gains in student learning and close the achievement gap
▷ Hold self and other adults accountable for ensuring high academic achievement for every student

Personal Responsibility and Relentless Drive

▷ Hold self personally accountable for outcomes and results
▷ Demonstrate relentless drive and determination to achieve outcomes and results
▷ Exhibit willingness to engage in difficult conversations and make hard decisions
▷ Exhibit resilience to overcome setbacks and remain constructive despite resistance or failure
▷ Lead in a way that reflects stated values and beliefs
▷ Demonstrate a commitment to urban school leadership and management

Results Orientation

▷ Has a track record of achieving goals and results
▷ Demonstrate and maintain a focus on goals and results
▷ Demonstrate resourcefulness to achieve goals and results
▷ Demonstrate willingness and ability to adjust strategies and practices in order to reach goals

Teaching And Learning

Knowledge of Teaching and Learning

▷ Demonstrate ability to drive dramatic improvements in academic achievement for all students
▷ Provide evidence of ability to align objectives and instructional activities to students' academic goals
▷ Understand and use a variety of instructional strategies to meet students' diverse learning needs
▷ Assess student learning and use data to guide and modify instruction
▷ Provide clear feedback to students and guide students in assessing their own learning
▷ Demonstrate the ability to distinguish among poor, mediocre, solid and outstanding teaching
▷ Articulate clear and compelling instructional expectations for classroom settings

Strategic Management

Problem Solving

▷ Identify, analyze and prioritize complex problems and key issues
▷ Analyze and diagnose complex issues
▷ Develop a strategic plan with concrete outcomes
▷ Develop effective solutions
▷ Demonstrate ability to evaluate results and use data to drive decision making

Project Management to Deliver Results

▷ Articulate a clear vision and goals
▷ Able to manage time effectively, prioritize, and organize strategies to reach goals
▷ Multi-task and balance detailed steps with the big picture to ensure successful project completion
▷ Delegate decision-making and authority in an effective manner
▷ Monitor a project by assessing milestones and modify plans based on data.

Leadership Qualities

Adult Leadership

▶ Mobilize adults to take action toward common goals

▶ Develop clear direction and shared purpose that guides and unifies the team

▶ Engage and empower others to take responsibility to achieve results

▶ Make clear decisions while considering diverse perspectives to reach the best solutions

▶ Demonstrate the ability to teach other adults and commit to adults' growth and development

▶ Build effective teams to meet the needs of the task

Communication and Listening

▶ Clearly articulate point of view, ideas and rationale

▶ Possess written and verbal skills to communicate in a clear and concise manner, which is appropriate for and understood by intended audiences

▶ Demonstrate poise, confidence and professionalism in diverse situations

▶ Actively listen to and engage with others

▶ Possess a leadership voice; inspire and lead through communication and presence

Interpersonal Skills

▶ Successfully build relationships

▶ Promote diversity in communication, understanding and engagement

▶ Treat every adult and student with respect, dignity and understanding

▶ Diffuse anger and find common ground to move people toward solutions

▶ Exhibit confidence, competence and a sense of possibility, including when under pressure

▶ Accurately read group dynamics to maximize individual strengths

Self-Awareness and Commitment to Ongoing Learning

▶ Accurately identify technical and interpersonal strengths and areas for development

▶ Reflect on experiences to grow and develop

▶ Seek feedback and take action to develop personally and professionally

▶ Demonstrate humility and willingness to continually improve

▶ Demonstrate awareness of impact on and perception by others

Path to Principalship

SOURCE: **Gwinnett County Public Schools Quality-Plus Leader Academy**

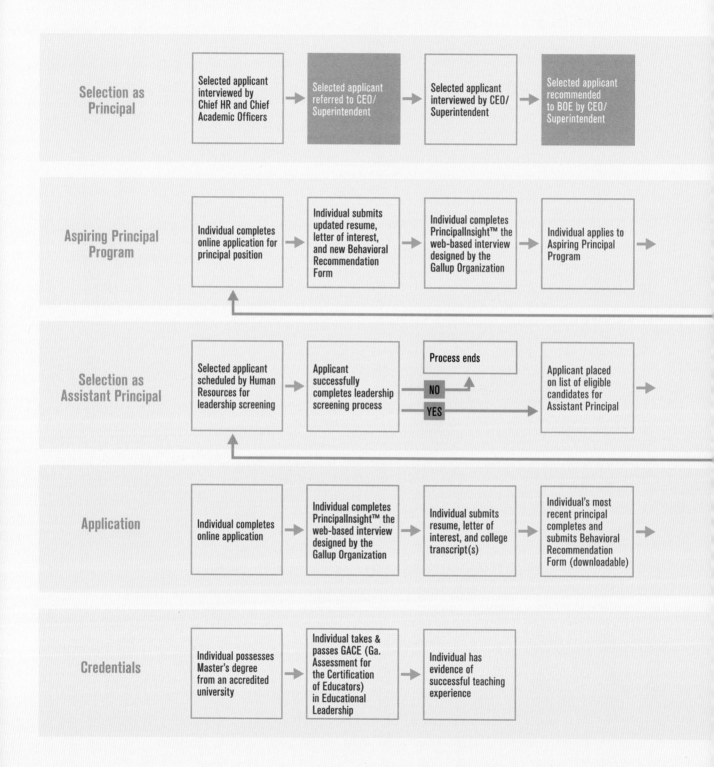

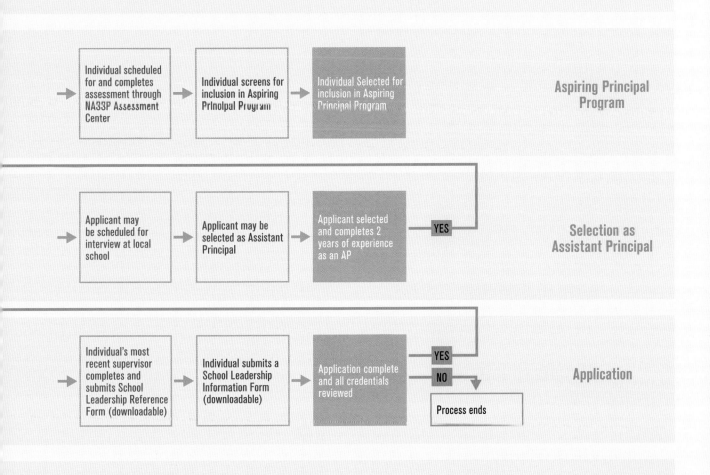

Selection as Principal

Aspiring Principal Program

Individual scheduled for and completes assessment through NA33P Assessment Center → Individual screens for inclusion in Aspiring Principal Program → Individual Selected for inclusion in Aspiring Principal Program

Selection as Assistant Principal

Applicant may be scheduled for interview at local school → Applicant may be selected as Assistant Principal → Applicant selected and completes 2 years of experience as an AP — YES

Application

Individual's most recent supervisor completes and submits School Leadership Reference Form (downloadable) → Individual submits a School Leadership Information Form (downloadable) → Application complete and all credentials reviewed — YES / NO → Process ends

Credentials

Leadership Screening Fact Sheet

SOURCE: **Gwinnett County Public Schools Quality-Plus Leader Academy**

Gwinnett County Public Schools' (GCPS) vision for leadership states that our "Quality-Plus" leaders focus on results. They lead by example, energize others, and execute plans that turn vision into reality. They promote a performance culture by helping other employees see how their work contributes to excellence in teaching and learning. Lifelong learners, they continually improve their own performance so that the organization continues to improve, and accept responsibility for effective communication of the system's direction.

As one of Gwinnett County Board of Education Strategic Goals for the school system, GCPS is committed to recruit, employ, develop, and retain a workforce that achieves the mission and goals of the organization. In order to achieve this goal, Gwinnett County Public School employs a rigorous screening process for prospective leaders. The purpose of leadership screening is to assess leadership skills and behaviors that are essential to being an effective leader in GCPS.

The process consists of four levels.

LEVEL 1
Credential review

▶ Completed application
▶ 2 references
▶ PrincipalInsight™—Web-based assessment
▶ Georgia leadership certificate

LEVEL 2
Written Exercise

▶ Computer-based written in-basket exercise

LEVEL 3
Structured Interview

▶ 60-minute interview with a Panel of GCPS Leaders

LEVEL 4
Approved Applicant

▶ List After successful completion of the structured interview, an applicant's name will be placed on an approved list for employment.

Leadership is the fundamental element in creating a coherent organization that is capable of achieving and sustaining phenomenal success. The Gwinnett County Public Schools' Leadership Development Team is dedicated to recruiting, employing, developing, and retaining highly qualified leaders to meet the needs of a growing student population.

Protocol for the Classroom Instruction Video

SOURCE: **University of Illinois at Chicago**

Our purpose in viewing this videotape with you is to get a better sense of how you view classroom instruction and how you might communicate your views to teachers. There is no single correct way to interpret what you will see in this video; there are multiple ways to interpret what is going on in the classroom. We want to hear your interpretation.

Scenario: Assume that one of your practices as a principal is the "3-minute walkthrough." Your purpose in visiting several classes a day for 2-4 minutes at a time is NOT to give immediate feedback to the teacher, but to get a sense of what is going on in classrooms in the school as a whole, so you can talk to the entire faculty, or to grade level teams, about what you are seeing and engage them in conversations about teaching. After viewing a teacher on multiple occasions, you may choose to have an individual conversation with that teacher, and you would schedule a more in-depth visit after having such a one-on-one conversation.

This tape, however, is a record of your visiting the classroom 6 or 7 times, as you gather your thoughts about instructional issues it raises for discussion with the teaching staff in general and with this teacher in particular.

Questions for you to ponder as you view this tape:

1. What did you like, and not like, about the samples of classroom instruction you observed in several visits to this classroom?

2. What instructional issues arise for you, positive and negative, that you think may be worth discussing with the teaching staff in general in the school (and how would you frame such issues in raising them for staff discussion)?

3. What instructional issues arise for you that you think are worth discussing with the teacher as an individual, both to get a better understanding of what she is doing and to provide feedback to her? Taking those issues into account:

    a. What questions do you have for this teacher?
    b. What kind of feedback would you be willing to give her at this point?
    c. What would you most be looking for if you did a one-hour in-depth observation of this teacher's teaching? Why?
    d. No matter how strong or weak this teacher's teaching, what strategies would you employ to help this teacher continue to develop her effectiveness? What further learning or professional development would you need to do as an administrator to provide the best possible support for this teacher's development?

Facilitated Group Interview

SOURCE: **NYC Leadership Academy**

General Directions Approximate time, want to learn about how you approach problems, put self in place of the principal, don't use "what my principal did", ask questions if you don't understand directions, there is not a specific correct answer, take notes if that is your style, notes not collected

PART ONE Read the scenario and give directions to participants.
You are placed in April as the principal of a mid-size NYC public school. The previous principal was removed after serving as the head of the school for 9 months.

The school serves an ethnically diverse population of students, mainly from low-income families. The majority of your students are scoring at levels 2 and 3 on standardized tests. However, few students, regardless of performance level, are making one year of progress. Your new network leader tells you that the school's inquiry team studied this problem and discovered that the students in the self contained special education classes seemed to be struggling the most with making progress. The team recommended going to a CTT model as the best way to support those students as well as the overall statistics for the school. The network leader tells you that he sees some merit in this but it is your decision to make.

What are the implications of implementing this model? What concerns you the most?
5 minutes reflection, 10 minutes discussion

What additional information do you want to have before making this decision? How will your get it?
Discussion is immediate, 5 minutes

The next sections are for facilitator only. You are to read the pieces of the scenario and the participants will have to take notes on whatever information they see as important. Push on individual responses.

Based on the recommendation of the inquiry team and the additional information you acquired you have decided to implement the CTT model for September.

What is your communication plan? Include the audience, the method as well as the main points of the message. Discussion is immediate, 10 minutes

The reactions you get from your decision are as follows:
- Parents of the students in the special education classes support it but are concerned
- Teachers are, for the most part, opposed to the change.
- Network leader is unhappy with the calls he is getting from the UFT and concerned parents
- OSEPO has decided to send you additional students who need self contained special education classes since you now have room

How do you feel about your decision now? What else might you have considered? Are there any adjustments you might make? Discussion is immediate, 5 minutes.

PART TWO **Read the scenario and give directions to participants.**

It is the first week of July. You wanted to include several items in your budget that you consider critical to the success of implementing the new model. You had some preliminary discussions with your staff, SLT and PTA. Unfortunately, your final budget is now in and is $120,000 less than what you planned on having available.

Item	Prior Spending & Rationale	Additional Relevant Data
Professional Development	This $75,000 program was designed to support teachers who are implementing the CTT model as well as all staff with differentiation of instruction.	The plan includes dollars for substitutes to allow for inter-visitation as well as per session dollars for planning and training.
Enrichment Programs	$25,000 was set aside for music and art consultants, $30,000 for after school and Saturday programs. $10,000 for instructional materials.	Many parents were concerned that the inclusion of special education students in the classroom would deny their children the attention they need to go beyond the basic curriculum. You guaranteed that you would set aside dollars for cultural programs after school and Saturdays as well as an art and music program.
Part time coordinator	This position was intended to alleviate some of the administrative burden caused by program change. Making sure IEPs were updated and all approvals accounted for as well as an analysis of students' needs are part of the job responsibilities.	The half time position was budgeted for $40,000 in salary and $12,000 in fringe benefits. This position was designed for a senior teacher who has been very supportive of the changes you are making and is viewed as a leader by the rest of the staff. You saw this as a way of beginning to distribute leadership in the school.

Which programs would you cut and why? You have 5 minutes to make your plan.
Discussion: 15 minutes

Ask the following questions. What did you consider in making your decision? Who would you have spoken with? What are the consequences of your decision and how will you deal with them?

Total interview time should not exceed 60 minutes.

Interview Schedule

SOURCE: **University of Illinois at Chicago**

Task	Description	Time Frame
Writing Prompt	Assessment of writing ability and administrative qualities. Interviewee is given a reading upon arrival and has to answer the 3 questions regarding leadership approach to issue.	45 minutes
Review of application materials	Panel of interviewers upon arrival are given packet of materials to review prior to interviewee coming into the room. Panelist should develop questions from materials as well review for any missing information.	10 minutes
Candidate Presentation & Questions	Candidate explains strategy for turning around a failing Chicago Public School. Interviewee was sent two case studies one grammar school and one high school they should pick one and develop a strategy for turning the failing school around in three years.	30 minutes
Video Review & Questions	Interviewees are informed upon arriving for the interview that they will watch a 5 minute video and be asked to: 1). Explain what you saw (instruction, classroom environment, etc). 2).What suggestions would you give the teacher regarding instruction, professional development and classroom environment. Provide recommendation for the teacher.	30 minutes
Review and Discuss Portfolio	Candidate should provide evidence of potential as a transformative instructional leader through pictures, artifacts and narrative. Portfolio structured in the Problem, Action, Result or Situation, Task, Action, Result format to show leadership, team building, communication skills. Must include copies of all certifications in the back of portfolio.	15 minutes
Final Q & A for Candidate	Panel of UIC coaches, mentors, and faculty will ask questions concerning the skills, abilities and qualities of the candidate as it relates to successful completion of the program.	15 minutes
Candidate Questions	Candidate has 10 minutes to ask any further questions regarding the program, UIC, the College of Education, faculty, etc.	5 minutes
Completing Rubric	Panelists complete individual rubrics and discuss candidate qualities.	15 minutes
Total time:	Two hours in interview room and 45 minutes prior to entering interview room for writing prompt.	2 hours and 45 minutes

Selection Criteria Rubric Sample

SOURCE: **New Leaders for New Schools**

RESULTS ORIENTATION Is the candidate focused on goals and results related to student achievement?

1	2	3	4
☐ Does not demonstrate any resourcefulness	☐ Struggles to demonstrate resourcefulness to achieve goals and results	☐ Sometimes demonstrates resourcefulness to achieve goals and results	☐ Demonstrates resourcefulness to achieve goals and results
☐ Is not willing to adjust strategies and practices to reach goals	☐ Is willing at times but struggles to adjust strategies and practices to reach goals; strategies may be ineffective	☐ Often adjusts strategies and practices in effective ways, when appropriate, to reach goals	☐ Consistently adjusts strategies and practices in effective ways, when appropriate, to reach goals
☐ Does not identify situations/ issues that require change and/or takes no action to make change	☐ Identifies situations/Issues that require change, but takes limited or highly ineffective action to initiate change	☐ Takes initiative that may result in positive change in the school, classroom, or work environment	☐ Takes initiative that results in lasting, positive change in the school, classroom, or work environment—the initiative reflects creativity and resourcefulness

Competency Scoring Sample

SOURCE: **University of Virginia Partnership for Leaders in Education**

Influence with the specific intent to increase the short and long-term effectiveness of another person.

1. Provides specific feedback, both positive and negative, to help others improve.

2. Expresses positive expectation for future performance after a setback, and either provides much more specific advice for tackling challenging assignments or provides negative feedback in specific not global terms.

3. Ensures that others obtain the experiences and training they need to develop new skills and levels of capability. Or gets others to fix problems and figure out solutions themselves. (Does not include signing off on required training.)

4. Gives full responsibility for very challenging work to others as "stretch" experiences, with full latitude for choosing work steps and making mistakes from which to learn. May promote others as a reward for development or as a developmental opportunity.

Sample Selection Matrix

	Resume screen	On-line application	Essays/ Written assessments (LOI)	References/ Recommendations	Commercial assessments	Phone Interview	In-person Interview	In basket exercise	Selection/ Group Interview Day	Leaderless Group Discussion	Video exercise	Role play
Belief and Urgency												
Personal Responsibility and Relentless Drive												
Results Orientation												
Adult Leadership												
Interpersonal Skills												
Teaching and Learning												
Self-awareness												
Communication and Listening												
Problem Solving												

APPENDIX E

Training and Developing Fellows

Residency Compact

SOURCE: NYC Leadership Academy

The purpose of the Residency Compact is to outline the Leadership Academy's expectations for the mentor principals and the Aspiring Principals during the residency year. It is our expectation that the mentor principals will share, think-through and provide opportunities for participants to practice the skills necessary to be effective instructional and transformational leaders. The following activities have been assigned by the Academy:

- Complete a *minimum* of one written classroom observation per week, one of which must be with the mentor principal and conducted on a monthly basis;
- Complete a *minimum* of three walk-throughs with the mentor principal per semester that focus on student learning;
- Participate in the CFI Inquiry team;
- Participate in the Quality Review Process;
- Participate in or start an additional school-based team or committee with an instructional or operational focus;
- Participate in reflective debriefs with the mentor principal;
- Maintain a portfolio that reflects key learnings of the residency;
- Develop and complete a comprehensive school-specific residency project aligned to the instructional needs of the school.

By the end of the residency year, the Aspiring Principal must demonstrate leadership stance and a working knowledge and implications of standards, instruction, assessment, and curriculum design.

In addition to his/her responsibilities at the residency site, it is the Academy's expectation that the Aspiring Principal complete all Academy assignments; attend all Tuesday and Thursday Academy sessions and participate in the Residency switch.

Learning Goals of Aspiring Principal

This Compact also provides an opportunity for the Aspiring Principal to identify and outline individual learning goals and objectives for the duration of the internship. All learning goals align with NYC Leadership Performance Matrix and NYC School Leadership Competencies.

In addition to the aforementioned expectations, the Aspiring Principal should identify and map personal learning goals for the residency year. Specific activities that will focus on these goals should be developed and listed on page 2 of this document. Activities in the residency should address learning goals in the areas of: **Curriculum and Instruction (C)**, **Supervision of Instruction (S)**, and **Administration (A)**. The learning goals outlined in the **Leadership (L)** area must be demonstrated in all aspects of the work undertaken by the Aspiring Principal.

Residency Compact continued

Area		Learning Goal	
A*	Leadership (L)	1.0	Personal Behavior
		2.0	Resilience
		3.0	Communication
		5.0	Situational Problem-Solving
		10.0	School Climate and Culture
B/C*	Curriculum and Instruction (C)	4.0	Focus on Student Performance
		6.0	Learning
D*	Supervision of Instruction (S)	7.0	Accountability for Professional Practice
		8.0	Supervision of Instructional and Non-instructional staff
		9.0	Leadership Development
E*	Administration (A)	11.0	Time/Task/Project Management
		12.0	Technology

*NYC Core Competencies: (A) Personal Leadership, (B) Use of Data, (C) Curriculum & Instruction, (D) Development of Staff, (E) Use of Resources

Specific Activities Aligned to Learning Goals

INSTRUCTIONS: The mentor principal and the Aspiring Principal should collaboratively establish specific activities to be accomplished in order to meet the Aspiring Principal's learning goals.

Area	Activities	
1 (C)	a	
	b	
	c	
	d	
	e	
2 (S)	a	
	b	
	c	
	d	
	e	
3 (A)	a	
	b	
	c	
	d	
	e	

A NEW APPROACH TO PRINCIPAL PREPARATION

© 2008 by NYC Leadership Academy, Inc., Long Island City, NY. All rights reserved.

Agreement & Signatures

A. The Aspiring Principal, mentor principal, and NYCLA strand facilitator will review the progress made on this compact and modify as necessary for the purpose of ensuring that the terms have been or will be met before the conclusion of the 2009–2010 residency year.

B. As an Aspiring Principal, I agree that I have identified the skills and competencies stated in the compact and will undertake the specific activities outlined in this compact in order to meet these learning goals. I also agree to support the learning goals of my residency partner (if applicable), the NYC Leadership Academy strand network team and the activities my partner and team will undertake to meet their goals over the course of the residency year.

_____

Aspiring Principal (Signature)

_____

Aspiring Principal (Print Name)   Date

C. As a mentor principal, I agree to support, collectively and individually, the Aspiring Principal(s) named above in performing the specific activities outlined in this compact in order to achieve their learning goals during the 2009–2010 residency year.

_____

Mentor Principal (Signature)

_____

Mentor Principal (Print Name)   Date

D. NYCLA Strand Facilitator

_____

NYCLA Strand Facilitator (Signature)

_____

NYCLA Strand Facilitator (Print Name)   Date

Individual Learning Plan Summary Document

SOURCE: **New Leaders for New Schools**

Five Standards:

1. **Learning and Teaching:** The New Leader drives a rigorous curriculum aligned with high standards, delivered through research-based, data-driven instructional practices, and informed by robust assessment to achieve targeted student learning goals.

2. **School Culture:** The New Leader inspires a vision and builds relationships with parents, staff, and the community to create a culture that advances the belief that all children can achieve at high levels and that all adults are responsible for student achievement.

3. **Aligning Staff:** The New Leader ensures the recruitment, selection, development, and evaluation of a staff that is aligned with the vision and philosophy about learning, teaching and culture that drives dramatic gains in student achievement.

4. **Systems and Operations:** The New Leader implements, maintains, and monitors operations and systems to support learning and school culture that drives dramatic gains in student achievement.

5. **Personal Leadership:** The New Leader takes responsibility to set a personal example, demonstrates self-awareness, builds trust, and maintains an urgent, relentless focus on student achievement.

The coach and New Leader develop an individual learning plan using the following template:

	Areas for Growth	Next Steps	Timeline	Evidence
Learning and Teaching				
School Culture				
Aligning Staff				
Systems and Operations				
Personal Leadership				

Summer Intensive Themes

SOURCE: **NYC Leadership Academy**

	Weekly Themes
Week 1	**Orientation/Analysis of Data** How do we look at schools? What data do we select? How is the organization of data an expression of one's mental model?
Week 2	**Standards, Curriculum and Assessments** How do we take a deeper look at the school? What additional information do we need and how do we use it to support student learning?
Week 3	**The Social Context of Schooling** How do we assess and understand the school tone, culture and climate? How do we understand systems thinking in the context of the school?
Week 4	**Resource Allocation/Managing Vision** How do we organize money, people, time and structures to articulate and support the school vision?
Week 5	**Capacity Building** How do we leverage assets to develop staff in order to improve student learning? Where do we want to go? Where do we begin? How do you get there?
Week 6	**Transition to a New Role/Entering Residency** How do I make the shift? How do I address the needs of my school as well as my own learning needs?

Summer Intensive Sample Days

SOURCE: **NYC Leadership Academy**

Activity	Mini-Lessons (Purpose, What Are We Doing And Why)
Monday, July 19 Day 10 9am-3pm	
AM Connections Frame for Week 3	Debrief leads into frame for week 3: Political/Social/Cultural/Economic context of schooling and how they play out in schools.
Stand by My Quote Activity	Stand by My Quote Activity Purpose: To articulate and share beliefs about the impact of classroom language on student learning. Quotes are taken from readings for the day; one posted in each corner of the room. Participants stand by the quote that resonates with them. Group shares out why they congregated around a specific quote.
Academic Language	Mini lesson: Academic Language Strand watches teacher video of Ryan Franklin. Participants should take low inference notes on teacher observation video. The goal here is to challenge participants' mental models of what a satisfactory lesson looks like. Debrief: ▷ If you were Principal would you hire this teacher? ▷ As a parent would you want this to be your child's teacher? ▷ What if Ryan Franklin were a white male or white female would you rate the lesson differently? ▷ Is engagement synonymous with learning? ▷ Who is using Academic Language?
Introduce Progress Report- Parent Presentation Assignment	Introduce Assignment – Explain Progress Report to Parents and review rubric and assignment expectations.
PM School Analysis feedback	Purpose: To help participants see how the same data may lead to different conclusions and the way values inform data analysis. Set up: fishbowl (2 reps from each project team form an inner circle, the rest form an outer circle) OR cross-project team share (half of project team presents to a visiting half of project team or carousel).Take on the role of a principal and present findings. Participants are responsible for presenting in "one voice." Assignment conversations: all participants engage in rigorous conversations about their data driven analysis. The rationale and justifications must come from available data. This activity allows participants to practice being concise, present data to an audience, highlight data to make a point, present a hypothesis with supporting evidence, and look at data in different ways. Participants need to think about whether or not they need a visual to support their data. Who will present? How are they going to present the information? Facilitators should ensure the analysis is steeped in the challenge of the scenario school Guiding questions: ▷ What data sources have you considered and/or have you not looked at? ▷ What evidence did you consider to support your conclusions? (quantitative, context) ▷ What are you learning from triangulating the data? (points of leverage) ▷ Has it led to the identification of leverage points? ▷ Use the ladder of inference (mental models) to evaluate the conclusions your peers made. ▷ Were there points at which conclusions were based on assumptions? ▷ Did the analysis confirm/disconfirm what was thought/found earlier? ▷ What judgments/values guided your peers' decision-making? Focus debrief on the way values inform data analysis and prioritization. ▷ How do you account for differences in the conclusions between the two principals?
Project Team Work	Project Team Work

THEME FOR WEEK 3 Focuses On The Following Ideas: The Social Context Of Schooling

How Do We Assess And Understand The School Tone, Culture And Climate?

How Do We Understand Systems Thinking In The Context Of The School?

Readings	HW	Notes	C.C.
Aronson, J. (2004). *The Threat of Stereotype.* Delpit, L.D. (1988). The Silenced Dialogue: Power and Pedagogy in Teaching Other People's Children. Johnston, P. (2004). *Choice words: How our language Affects Children's Learning* (chapters 1 & 3) Nakkula, M. (2003). *Identity and Possibility: Adolescent Development and Potential of School.* Pittman, K. (2003). *Some Things Do Make a Difference and We Can Prove it.* Tatum, B. (2007). *Can We Talk About Race* (pp. 39-57). Fullan, M. (2009). *The Challenge of Change: Start School Improvement Now! 2nd Ed.* Thousand Oaks, CA: Corwin Press. (pp 121-123).	School Analysis & Presentation (project team) Letter to Staff (individual) Group Work Plan (project team) Literature Review on Systems		(A) (B) (D)

Summer Intensive Sample Days continued

Activity	Mini-Lessons (Purpose, What Are We Doing And Why)
Tuesday, July 20 Day 11 9am-3pm	
AM Connections	
Starpower	Starpower Activity (Refer to Facilitator's handbook)
	Purpose: (1) To help participants see how they're influenced by power. (2) In order to change behavior, it may be necessary to first change the system.
	Debrief: What can be learned from this experience? In what ways did issues of race, class and other socioeconomic biases/barriers surface?
Writing prompt	**Facilitator's Choice:** Facilitator may want to use a writing prompt prior to the debrief if the room is very charged. It enables participants to have an individualized reflection period. How does this play out in schools? What are the challenges of leadership?

Readings	HW	Notes	C.C.
Barnes, N. (2000). Teaching Locations (chapter 11).	360° feedback	**Role Plays**	(A)
Bernard, B. (2003). Fostering Resiliency in Urban Schools.		Role Play offers participants a chance to inhabit, and to experiment with different ways of inhabiting a future professional role-in our case, that of a principal.	(D)
Hu, W. (2009). No Longer Letting Scores Separate Pupils.		**Scenarios:**	
McGrath, D., & Kuriloff, P. (1999). "They're Going to Tear the Doors Off This Place": Upper-middle Class Parent School Involvement and the Educational Opportunities of Other People's Children.		▷ Politically connected parent ▷ Parent that doesn't speak English ▷ Wealthy parent who's moving into the neighborhood and looking for a good school	
Noguera, P. (2008). The Trouble With Black Boys: And Other Reflections on Race, Equity, and the Future of Public Education. (chapter 6).		▷ Parent of little means whose child scored level 4 on the ELA and Math assessments ▷ Parent who wants to give a gift or a check to the principal because he wants to ensure that his child continues to receive a good education	
Sobel, A., & Gale Kugler, E. (2007). "Building Partnerships with Immigrant Parents".			

Foundational Year Scope & Sequence

SOURCE: **New Leaders for New Schools**

	June	July	August	September	October	November
Learning & Teaching						
Curriculum aligned to both state and college-readiness standards		Nat'l standards in lit & math	Curricular frameworks for district & state standards	District Grade level expectations for each grade/	What is being taught and what planning practices are there in Res sight	Gap analysis measuring current state and desired state–incl cultural biases
				Build capacity of others in unpacking standards, identifying mastery objectives, determining evidence of mastery, and planning instruction.		
Consistent and quality classroom practices, routines, and teaching strategies		RBT KB, Content specific strategies in literacy/num, Coaching/leading teachers for rigor	What are the practices that the districts recommends, Local teacher eval system, teacher obs/analysis contracts	obs/analysis beginning of year–starting school right, informal observations begin, Assessing Teacher Competency–Developmental stages of teachers, launching Mastery Case Study work	Clarity, CEIJ, Conferencing, monitoring, expectations/ linking formative assessment w/ student outcomes, (mock?) "formal" observations begin including pre/post conf-red flags for MP	Action plan for problem teachers, finalizing Mastery Case Study work
				Constantly observing classroom instruction, Workshopping Teacher Evaluations and conferencing w/cohort		
Utilization of diverse student-level data to drive instructional improvement		DDI cycle, rubric to gauge implementation of model, Assess the quality of aligned interim assessments, diagnose problematic planning/execution	Local assessment cycle, what are the data sources, platforms, types of questions, schedule for returns on data, digging into Res site data	Determine status of DDI at Res site (including disag, AYP, staff knowledge, etc) developing data team, data calendar and assessment prep plan	Barriers, Interim Assessments driver of rigor, deep Interim Assessments, Data displays, setting performance goals w/team	Looking at student work, assignments,
Individual and common planning for effective instruction		Decision making and consensus building, using data for collaborative planning		Backwards design–translating standards into daily instruction	Establishing expectations, building capacity, monitoring collaborations	Aligning Resources and Options to support individual planning.
Pyramid of academic interventions			District policies for intervention, IDEA, ELL-implementation, assessment	Use disaggregate data to determine needs of students, MP's implementation of IDEA, ELL policies	Use LT to engage others in IDing students needing intervention, Use data, budget, resources, student work to plan interventions for ind students	Collect and process data on success of plan

December	January	February	March	April	May	Learning & Teaching
What resources/ experts are in the district to support P to close gaps	Learn about stages of curricular implementation		How do you monitor a curriculum?	Action planning		Curriculum aligned to both state and college-readiness standards
Build capacity of others in unpacking standards, identifying mastery objectives, determining evidence of mastery, and planning instruction.						
Deep dive on RBT knowledge base, Launching Expectations Case Study		Observing and processing formal eval	Establishing common practices and expectations for all teachers– including beginning of year, finalizing Expectations Case Study	Discipline, principals of learning & leadership		Consistent and quality classroom practices, routines, and teaching strategies
Constantly observing classroom instruction, Workshopping Teacher Evaluations and conferencing w/cohort						
Reflecting on their own performance and that of team, comparing school process w/district process		Fixing gaps in DDI cycle within small cohort of teachers, naming gaps in the school	Addressing gaps in school	DDI model– planning Res site school improvement for next year	Time Mgmt, DDI culture, action, assessment, difficult conversations, Collecting data and determining next steps for team	Utilization of diverse student-level data to drive instructional improvement
	Holding teachers accountable for high quality planning				Scheduling for Common Planning	Individual and common planning for effective instruction
Building spirit of evidence and accountability for adults in intervention plans	Differentiated learning needs and systems for special education students	Teaching Teachers to use Action Research to provide intervention, collect data, assess effectiveness			Year end analysis of data	Pyramid of academic interventions
		Establish and use benchmarks for assessing effectiveness of interventions and sharing out w/ Leadership Team/ team of teachers				

Foundational Year Scope & Sequence continued

	June	July	August	September	October	November
Culture						
Adults and students champion school vision and mission		Culture vs climate	District indicators of school culture, analyze school vision/mission statement to see what is written that sets up culture	Best practices for orienting students, 1st week of school, establishing routines/rituals	Collect evidence that vision and mission is alive and well (or not), determine high impact actions to improve culture (high expectations/achievement in cohort of S&T,	
Adults demonstrate personal responsibility for student connection and student success		Steven Jones, Jeff Howard–social justice–tone, expectations, advocacy. Youth Development intensive for secondary.	Assess beliefs, relationships in Residency site–explore whether beliefs/tone/is reflected in contract, job descriptions, or teacher eval system (what is said and not said in these docs)	Launching belief work, Assess tone of school, structures for adult-student interaction, Establishing structures and supports for adult/student relationships	Dimensions/Components of School Culture–4 Frames, Sources of Authority, etc monitoring burgeoning relationships and problem solving–connect w/RBT KB expectations, class climate, personal relationship building–connect w/Expectations case study	
Adults and students live a code of conduct aligned to the school's vision, mission, and values		5 keys for effective school culture, guided discipline vs punishment, disc strategies	District policies on student discipline, due process, students' rights/responsibilities, attendance, suspension (including special ed)	Best practices for orienting students, first week of school, orienting new teachers, Determine Residency site school discipline policy.	Observation & feedback regarding discipline, mgmt, and tone (connect w/RBT KB–areas: Space, Time, Routines, Momentum, Discipline)	Gap Analysis (including Data) comparing school discipline policy, process, appeals, etc w/ideal state (accountable, supportive, school-wide)
Adults insist and support students in having high aspirations for themselves		Social, emotional devel–YD	District policies for social/emotional support/intervention	Social/emotional needs and developmental appropriate strategies/structures Kids owning their own behavior, connect to RBT attribution retraining, 20 ways to communicate high expectations	Plan for students to set personal goals for achievement	Implementing system for monitoring and problem solving around student self-perceptions
Families engaged in supporting their child's/youth's learning, conduct, and college/career planning			District policy concerning parent involvement, homeless context in city–district policy	Best practices for parent engagement including–who are they, options for engagement, motivators for engagement, etc (Joyce Epstein, Anne Henderson, Met Life Engaging Parents, Family, Community)		Supporting and monitoring teacher engagement w/parents, best practices homelessness/social emotional crisis intervention (substance abuse, domestic violence, etc)

December	January	February	March	April	May	Culture
Implementing action plan, collecting evidence, problem solving, building capacity of teachers			Reflect on learnings and takeaways–how to apply when principal?			Adults and students champion school vision and mission
Assessment of cohort relationships– sharing out in weekly meetings	Reflecting on learnings from work w/ cohort relationships– prioritize key actions/ obstacles			Develop action plan for implementation share out at weekly meetings		Adults demonstrate personal responsibility for student connection and student success
monitoring burgeoning relationships and problem solving– connect w/RBT KB expectations, class climate, personal relationship building–connect w/Expectations case study						
Robert Debruyn–tools for principal as disciplinarian–last stop, de-escalating (not escalating)/ Developmentally appropriate best practices				Continuing to close gaps in current system, assessing remaining learning needs		Adults and students live a code of conduct aligned to the school's vision, mission, and values
Trouble-shooting around student self-perceptions				Reflection-prioritizing high impact actions and plans for next year		Adults insist and support students in having high aspirations for themselves
Supporting and monitoring teacher engagement w/parents, best practices homelessness/social emotional crisis intervention (substance abuse, domestic violence, etc)		Reflecting on what worked, learning strategies from colleagues		Developing a plan for parent engagement		Families engaged in supporting their child's/youth's learning, conduct, and college/career planning

Foundational Year Scope & Sequence continued

	June	July	August	September	October	November
Aligned Staff						
Recruitment, selection, and placement of aligned staff			District job descriptions,	Selection/Rec. practices at Res site, ID	Recruiting/ Selection strategies	Gap analysis and plan for improvement
Consistent feedback and professional learning drive instructional improvement		CEIJ, Systemic Expectations and Feedback		characteristics of quality feedback (timely, descriptive, data generated, objective)/ Diagnosing Teacher Learning Needs	Practice/Reflection on Feedback Strategies/Mastery Case Study	Novice/Vet, Open/ Resistant, role of age in feedback dynamics
Monitoring and management of staff performance		RBT OAT, identifying systemic expectations, non-negotiables, ▸ Build capacity of the LIA team ▸ Build the capacity of other	Evaluation cycles, how to fire teachers. Metro Princ: What power will Res have to manage staff (e.g., union contract, HR, Union)? Establish team with whom they'll be working.	Stating expecta- tions, enforcing expectations, molding, examining MP practice to articulate & moni- tor expectations (gap analysis)	Using RBT observation & supervision to manage teachers, create individual teacher profiles– management & support	Process & performance check–enough power, enough skill? Review of contract–district lawyer, others re legalities
High-performing instructional leadership team (HPILT)	▸ characteristics, practices, and stages of HPLT ▸ Plan and lead meetings using FL ID LT members in LIA	LT interaction with other teams & structures, stages of team development	How this team operates/interacts w/other teams in building. Avoid being subsumed by governance	Launching LT in small cohort/ articulating vision for team	FL strategies applied and processed	Assessing RPR Progress and processing w/ LT and then NL colleagues

December	January	February	March	April	May	Aligned Staff
Gap analysis and plan for improvement	Interview questions	Recruitment strategies, materials		Job Design, Recuiting, Selection	Job design/org chart workshop	Recruitment, selection, and placement of aligned staff
	Launch recruitment/selection for residency site or own school if placed					
Holding Teachers Accountable to Professional Development Learning–Stage 4 Guskey–are they applying what they've learned w/ quality & fidelity?	Informal Teacher Development Opportunities	CEIJ Conversations		360 Feedback Cycle at Residency site & Reflection	Difficult Conversations	Consistent feedback and professional learning drive instructional improvement
Pick a problem teacher and "participate" in formals (mock evals, etc)			"Participate" as MP counsels out or removes un-aligned teacher (follow the process closely)	Cohort-processing reviewing the learnings of contractual process–removal of teachers	Final Reflection	Monitoring and management of staff performance
Making Adjustments, monitoring progress on RPR					Plan for LT in residency site next year–sustainability post-resident/ plans for LT in principalship	High-performing instructional leadership team (HPILT)

Foundational Year Scope & Sequence continued

	June	July	August	September	October	November
Systems and Operations						
Tracking of clear and focused school goals and strategy adjustment based on progress		Diagnostic Tool	Assess existing School Improvement Plan–process w/NL cohort: alignment of HR, budget, resources, stakeholders, etc, Diagnostic tool applied to residency site		w/MP: Action plan for Res site including goals for cohort of students, benchmarks, re-evaluate against budget, resources, early results, etc., connecting work of teacher cohort to school improvement plan–team achievement goals for year. (Math & Literacy projects)	
			Gap Analysis Between Diagnostic and School Improvement Plan		Use Diagnostic Tool on School Visits	
Time use aligned to school-wide goals			Pd requirements in district/contract/state teacher planning, seat time for students, max teaching time, out of content teaching, curricular teaching-time requirements	Assessing time on different content areas, time on task in instruction, adult collaboration structures	Maximizing instructional time–scheduling secrets (Joplan, block scheduling, etc)	Collaborative adult times, Data, Dialogue, Decision Making, how to navigate the contract–maximizing time w/teachers,
				w/LT, build calendar mapping assessments, academic interventions, PD, team mtgs, etc		drivers and inhibitors to maximizing instruction
Budget, external partnerships, and facilities aligned to strategic plan			Assess school budget w/NL cohort, building relationship and engaging around budget with governance board/school improvement team,etc (stakeholder/decision makers around budget)		Gap Analysis of budget to school improvement plan	Make suggestions to the MP on aligning budget and other resources to goals
Political context and school system relationships managed to ensure a focus on learning			Local Politics, Agendas, Identify key players in school/district/neighborhood, navigating district org chart	The Political Frame, attend district/governance board meeting and identify topics, implications, players, etc/existing MP process to engage community in vision/goals for school, gap analysis of current engagement dynamics		Meeting w/community leaders, district leader, report out on political frame in practice/negotiating landscape of all the players/decision makers in budgets and facilities/make recommendations to MP around ways to improve community/stakeholder engagement

December	January	February	March	April	May	Systems and Operations
w/ MP: Action plan for Res site including goals for cohort of students, benchmarks, re-evaluate against budget, resources, early results, etc., connecting work of teacher cohort to school improvement plan–team achievement goals for year. (Math & Literacy projects)	Strategies for maintaining focus on goals, examining benchmark data	Using data/data displays		Reflections/ Lessons Learned	Personal and School Goals for Principalship–make recommendations for significant changes to existing school improvement plan (School Improvement Plan project–if applicable)	Tracking of clear and focused school goals and strategy adjustment based on progress
Use Diagnostic Tool on School Visits						
Collect Data on Effectiveness of current school schedule	Monitoring success and useability of calendar	Gap Analysis of school calendar– plan for next year		Recommendations to MP about path to consistent whole-school schedule		Time use aligned to school-wide goals
drivers and inhibitors to maximizing instruction						
Budget planning for next year w/MP	Nuts and bolts of budget process	Unspoken, political, subtextual aspect of budget negotiations	identify strategic ways to use resources differently to meet school-wide student achievement goals at the residency site	Help MP to build the actual budget (if placed, map their own budget)	Budget, external partnerships, and facilities aligned to strategic plan
Meeting w/community leaders, district leader, report out on political frame in practice/negotiating landscape of all the players/decision makers in budgets and facilities/make recommendations to MP around ways to improve community/ stakeholder engagement	Select key coalition/ partnership to strengthen, begin representing school interests independently, problem solve w/ NL cohort	Unspoken, political, subtextual aspect of budget negotiations	4 Frames revisited	Lessons Learned, goal setting	Political context and school system relationships managed to ensure a focus on learning

	June	July	August	September	October	November
Personal Leadership						
Belief-based, Goal-driven Leadership: Leader consistently demonstrates belief in the potential of every student to achieve at high levels		Holding Adults Accountable for student Achievement, Efficacy		Assess Beliefs at Residency Site	Areas to Communicate Expectations, Attribution Retraining	Confronting Low Expectations, Changing Beliefs, Problem Solving w/NL Cohort
				Expectations Case Study		
Culturally Competent Leadership: Leader develops deep understanding of their urban context and actively moves the expectations of others in order to ensure high academic achievement for every student		Dynamics of Difference, Race/Culture/Poverty/Diversity Analyzing Culture, examining biases & privileges, expanding cultural knowledge, values & behaviors–policies & practices The 13 Skills	Demographics/racial/gender/sexuality/diversity issues in district/city	Demographics/diversity issues at residency site/ what are common excuses for/ trends in poor performance (related to race, culture, sexuality, gender, etc?)	Expanding cultural knowledge, fearlessness & compassion, Leading for Equity	Lead courageous conversations about diversity and culture, and especially about the historical inequities of race and class and how they relate to student learning at residency site
Interpersonal Skills, Facilitative Leadership: Leader builds relationships and facilitates active communities of adults and students dedicated to reaching school goals		Facilitative Leadership practices : building consensus, collaborative problem solving, team building, honoring each team member, Providing opportunities for and facilitate stakeholder group members to collaborate, exhibit and develop leadership, and guide the direction of the school Communicate effectively with all stakeholders, including listening actively and connecting conversations and meetings to school goals and values	Self assessment of interpersonal skill set	Assess interpersonal dynamics and group processes in residency site–sense of empowerment for individuals	Launch Facilitative Leadership Practices w/teacher cohort–problem solve and report out w/NL colleagues	
Adaptive Leadership: Leader drives and manages the organizational change process to increase student achievement		Balcony/dance floor, Zone of disequilibrium, "Protect Voices without Authority," "Give Work Back to the People," Pressure cooker, Ripening issues, "Work avoidance behavior," Regulate level of stress, Case in point protocol		Assess self and others-impact on student achievement. Assesses residency site challenges for root causes.	Difficult conversations List of adaptive challenges and list of technical challenges, introduces adaptive model to team, Identify other adaptive leaders	Application of 5 principals, leading broadly
Resilient Leadership: Leader demonstrates self-awareness, ongoing learning, and resiliency in the service of continuous improvement		In one on ones: identify personal strengths & areas of growth, establishes plan for growth (Assess: humility, flexibility, sensitivity, empathy, lack of egocentric approach)		Strategies and attitudes for feedback	Impact on others	Disappointments & setbacks–strategies for management

December	January	February	March	April	May		Personal Leadership
Confronting Low Expectations, Changing Beliefs, Problem Solving w/NL Cohort						Efficacy	Belief-based, Goal-driven Leadership: Leader consistently demonstrates belief in the potential of every student to achieve at high levels
Expectations Case Study							
Gap analysis of current state of all diversity issues in school/midpoint self-assessment on difficult conversations, biases, etc.	Solve for gaps					Expanding cultural knowledge	Culturally Competent Leadership: Leader develops deep understanding of their urban context and actively moves the expectations of others in order to ensure high academic achievement for every student
Launch Facilitative Leadership Practices w/teacher cohort–problem solve and report out w/NL colleagues							Interpersonal Skills, Facilitative Leadership: Leader builds relationships and facilitates active communities of adults and students dedicated to reaching school goals
Messenger and listener, decision making: ethics, values, & results		Technical vs adaptive revisited					Adaptive Leadership: Leader drives and manages the organizational change process to increase student achievement
	Matching leadership style to stage of school development	process of continuous improvement (data, dialogue, decision)					Resilient Leadership: Leader demonstrates self-awareness, ongoing learning, and resiliency in the service of continuous improvement

Residency Summary
SOURCE: KIPP School Leadership Program

Overview
The School Residencies place Fisher Fellows in high-performing KIPP, charter, traditional public, and private schools across the country to observe and participate in their leadership and operation. The School Residency experiences are customized to allow Fisher Fellows to focus on their own individualized leadership needs.

Goals
By participating in their School Residencies, participants will:

- Gain behind-the-scenes insight into the instructional, operational, and people management practices of successful school leaders
- Gather and synthesize ideas from high-performing schools to inform their own School Design Plans
- Reflect upon and implement learnings from Summer Institute and Intersessions in a school setting
- Contribute to the host school utilizing the leadership competencies outlined as strengths on their Individualized Leadership Plans (ILP)
- Take on roles and/or manage projects that allow them to practice the areas of development on their Individualized Leadership Plans
- Perform tasks and actively participate in the day-to-day instructional, operational, or people management of the host school
- Participate on the New School Site Visits review team for first year KIPP schools

KIPP Leadership Competencies
Residencies will be designed to address specific KIPP Leadership Competencies based on the Fisher Fellow's individual leadership strengths and areas for development.

Structure
Fisher Fellows typically complete 10 total weeks of Residencies in a variety of high-performing schools across the country. However, each Fisher Fellow will have an individualized residency plan that incorporates feedback from the Fisher Fellow Selection Interviews, input from the KSLP team, and recommendations from their Executive Director.

Residency Expectations
Fellows

- Meet with School Leader prior to the start of the first day onsite
- Set and refine Residency goals with host School Leader, using ILP as guide
- Determine how to best accomplish goals by developing a set of agreed upon outcomes
- Perform tasks that are aligned with individualized learning goals
- Integrate into the culture, activities, and daily life of the host school
- Share feedback with host site
- Be respectful of the culture, relationships, and systems in place at the school

School Leaders

- Meet with Fellow prior to the start of the first day onsite
- Review Fellow's Residency goals
- Determine how to best accomplish goals by developing a set of agreed upon outcomes
- Plan meaningful projects for Fellow to help him/her achieve learning goals
- Provide ongoing feedback to Fellow, meeting at least once per week to:
  - Discuss Fellow's key lessons learned and observations made
  - Provide Fellow with feedback and questions for reflection
  - Provide feedback via the ILP at end of residency

Recommendations on Identifying and Choosing Coaches

SOURCE: **Rainwater Leadership Alliance**

A first step is identifying the coaching talent pool. RLA programs focus on actively recruiting the right people for the complex job of coach. Potential talent pools used by RLA programs include:

▷ Recently retired principals within the target district or CMO that have the kind of experience and knowledge that you want to impart to fellows—and drove student achievement gains in their schools.
▷ External sources, like universities, other organizations or other districts
▷ Executive coaches, if the goal is for coaches to supplement training specifically on personal leadership
▷ Former executives like CEOs or EDs who know how to run organizations

Out of the available pool, RLA members thoughtfully select the best coaches. Finding the ideal coach is not easy. Coaches need to understand the challenges of the modern day principalship as well adult development. The coach ideally should recently have been a successful principal him or herself, and should receive training from your program. That said, just because someone was an effective principal does not mean they will be an effective coach. It is not helpful for a coach to always tell the fellow what to do, but instead a coach needs to be able to step back and let the fellow explore the issues, come to decisions, and make his or her own mistakes.

Prior success as a principal should not be the only factor in selecting a mentor principal or a coach. Some traits to look for in both are the following:

▷ Shares belief that all children can learn at high levels
▷ Generates trust; builds relationships
▷ Communicates effectively; explains thinking/decision-making
▷ Facilitates action and results (action-oriented)
▷ Has strong follow-through
▷ Has credibility among his/her peers
▷ Feels accountable for fellow success
▷ Collects, analyzes, and shares data effectively
▷ Demonstrates clear record of transforming K–12 student learning

APPENDIX F

Supporting Principals

Mentor Program Fact Sheet

SOURCE: Gwinnett County Public Schools Quality-Plus Leader Academy

New principals and assistant principals in Gwinnett County Public Schools are supported by mentors during their first two years. The Leader Mentor Program provides individualized support for new leaders through one-on-one meetings, small group support sessions, and just-in-time training on essential leadership topics.

Purposes of Mentoring
▷ To provide continuous, personalized support for new school leaders.
▷ To engage new leaders in learning about and understanding job expectations and responsibilities.
▷ To encourage the professional growth of new school leaders through the identification and implementation of research-based leadership strategies that have demonstrated a positive correlation with increased student achievement.
▷ To establish non-evaluative partnerships between new leaders and experienced leaders who have consistently demonstrated the characteristics of Quality-Plus Leaders.
▷ To enhance the interpersonal, leadership, and management skills of new leaders through opportunities for practice, analysis, and reflection.

Characteristics of Mentors
▷ Mentors have a proven track record of serving as effective principals.
▷ Mentors demonstrate the ability to understand and communicate how experience can serve as a guide.
▷ Mentors model principles of continuous learning and reflection.
▷ Mentors understand and are committed to the vision, mission and strategic goals of Gwinnett County Public Schools.
▷ Mentors strive to help others surpass their present level of performance.

Responsibilities of Mentors
▷ To provide guidance that aligns with the vision, mission, and strategic goals of Gwinnett County Public Schools.
▷ To facilitate opportunities for the ongoing leadership development of new leaders.
▷ To support new leaders through regular one-on-one meetings.
▷ To listen to the questions and concerns of new leaders in order to provide appropriate clarification and direction.
▷ To collaborate with new leaders as they analyze current challenges and formulate plans for school improvement.

Gwinnett County Public Schools • 437 Old Peachtree Rd, NW, Suwanee, GA, 30024 • 678-301-7267 • www.gwinnett.k12.ga.us • © Gwinnett County Public Schools. All Rights Reserved.

Summer Leadership Conference
SOURCE: Gwinnett County Public Schools Quality-Plus Leader Academy

CEO/Superintendent J. Alvin Wilbanks states: **"Stability, continuity, sustainability, consistency..."** For 33 years, the annual Summer Leadership Conference has been a signature piece of the leadership development focus in Gwinnett County Public Schools, and, in fact, our school system's culture. I would contend that this annual gathering is the single most important leadership development activity of our year and a key to GCPS' success. Summer Leadership gives us an opportunity to learn from distinguished, nationally known speakers, but, perhaps more importantly, from each other as our own "in-house experts" share best practices in choice sessions. This shared experience of our leadership team further supports our efforts as a coherent organization that is focused on our core business of teaching and learning."

Conference Detail
▷ The conference spans two and a half days of collaborative and intense learning.
▷ The conference is convened at The Instructional Support Center, Suwanee, Georgia.
▷ School principals, assistant principals, and district-level leaders participate each year, with attendance typically over 750.
▷ Nationally known and recognized experts present relevant and insightful keynotes each day of the conference.

Conference At-A-Glance
Over 85 choice sessions, developed and delivered by leaders and teachers focused on:
▷ Closing the Achievement Gap
▷ Continuous Quality Improvement
▷ Quality-Plus Teaching Strategies
▷ Safe, Secure, and Orderly Schools
▷ Using Assessment Results to Shape Instruction
▷ Development and Support of Staff

Representative Keynotes
▷ Dr. Robert Marzano, *"School Leadership that Works: From Research to Results"*
▷ Dr. Anthony Muhammad, *"Transforming School Culture"*
▷ Dr. John Antoinetti, *"The Engagement Cube: What's Engaging Today's Learners?"*
▷ Dr. Robert Barr, *"The Kids Left Behind: Catching Up the Underachieving Children of Poverty"*
▷ Kati Haycock, *"Improving Achievement and Closing Gaps Between Groups"*
▷ Dr. Victoria Bernhardt, *"Using Data to Improve Student Learning"*
▷ Dr. Mark Milliron, *"A New Generation of Learning: Diverse Students, Emerging Technologies, and a Sustainability Challenge"*

Sample Network Meeting Plan

SOURCE: **School Leaders Network**

Meeting Objectives
▶ Collaboratively identify a common problem of practice worded as a question focused on student learning

Pre-Work: Complete *A Data Picture of Our School*

Opening (30 minutes)
▶ Informal Unscheduled Relationship Building Time: Meet and Greet
▶ Formal Relationship Building Activity and Check-In
▶ Logistics: Announcements & Good News
▶ Re-Establish the Norms

Managing the Immediacy (30 minutes) Organize members into pairs with new principals paired with more experienced principals. Tell members that each person will have seven minutes to describe one pressing issue they are facing today. The second member will get three minutes to ask you clarifying questions. Concluding the questions, there will be five minutes of open discussion for problem solving, sharing or support. After completion, the process switches and the other person has time to process.

Developing Content Outcomes (80 Minutes) Share the objectives for today's meeting.

Ask members to review their theory of change. (A theory of change is a brief statement of how the practice of the principal leads to increases in learning and performance for students. The theory of change is created using a series of If/then statements.)

Ask members to get into groups of three with different people then they partnered with during the Managing the Immediacy Section. Give each member three index cards. Ask each member to share their recordings from the pre-work "A Data Picture of Our School." Ask members to also share their "soft data" represented in the ideas, opinions and perceptions of their team members (a.k.a. your craft knowledge) what they believe to be the greatest impediment to increased student achievement. Based on the data and the members' theory of change, have each individual member write one to three problems on index cards that once solved would be the greatest lever to student achievement.

Invite all members back together. Ask members to organize the index cards based on commonalities. What problems are alike? Move the similar problem together; student culture problems, teacher professional development problems, community building problems etc. Ask members to see what kinds of problems are most common for this group.

Tell members that "a problem of practice is a problem, formatted as a question, summarizing a situation related directly to student learning." The identified problem of practice may or may not align with the district initiatives. It will be the problem that we will seek to solve for one leader this year and seek to inform our own learning of this issue at each of our schools.

Get consensus from the group around the kind of problem that is most common to the group. Ask individual members to try to write a problem statement that is applicable to his or her school about this kind of problem. Ask members to answer: What problem are we trying to solve? What is nature of this problem? Is it adaptive or technical? Is it meaningful and significant? Would solving this problem be good for kids? Make sure the problem of practices is small enough to win, but large enough to matter.

Try to avoid these common pitfalls when crafting your network's problem of practice; being too vague or global, phrasing problems as causes, or phrasing problems as solutions.

These are examples of a problem of practice, formatted as a question:

▶ Can high expectations for student work be seen in class work and instruction?

▶ How is teacher planning time affecting classroom practice?

▶ Are the instructional strategies, lessons, and assessments used by the classroom teacher appropriately rigorous and sufficiently relevant?

▶ To what degree do faculty members have common expectations for student learning and a common framework for instruction?

▶ What evidence do we have that teachers practice according to the Open Court Reading teacher's manual?

▶ Why do we have significant variability in performance results on standardized tests in 9th grade math?

▶ Do all teachers have a positive attitude about all students' academic potential and social behavior?

▶ Do our teachers feel empowered and demonstrate the necessary skills to succeed in a multicultural environment?

Take a vote or use another consensus gathering strategy to decide on what problem of practice the group would like to study throughout the year.

Encourage your members to select a problem of practice that is a) focused on student learning and b) observable during instructional rounds. If members are drawn to things like parent participation or attendance, please suggest using the descriptive consultancy protocol at another meeting time outside of the inquiry process.

Dining (30 minutes) Encourage members to trade seats and sit next to someone that they want to connect with about their identified issue of immediacy.

Reflecting (30 minutes)

▶ Ask for deep listening. Present the poem "Mother to Son".

▶ Provide a moment of silence to journal as reflection. Ask, "How will solving this problem of practice as a group have impact on your learning? How will it have impact for students? How will you know?"

Closing (30 minutes)

▶ Wrap-up, summarize, debrief

▶ What are you taking away from this meeting?

▶ Session Critique: How did we do as a community of practice?

▶ Write Evaluations

Planning (10 minutes) Future Dates, Venues, Topic and Responsibilities

SLN recognizes the organic and synergistic nature of providing opportunities for quality learning. We appreciate the expertise of each facilitator and the development of each community of practice. With that in mind, the network meeting plans were designed to provide an illustration of what a network meeting could like as members move through different phases. These meeting plans are meant to be used with flexibility and balance to best meet the needs of members.

Just-in-Time Training Fact Sheet
SOURCE: Gwinnett County Public Schools Quality-Plus Leader Academy

Gwinnett County Public Schools' (GCPS) commitment to continuous quality improvement is embedded in the system's vision, mission, and strategic goals. The vision for leadership states that our "Quality-Plus" leaders focus on results. They lead by example, energize others, and execute plans that turn vision into reality. They promote a performance culture by helping other employees see how their work contributes to excellence in teaching and learning. Lifelong learners, they continually improve their own performance so that the organization continues to improve, and accept responsibility for effective communication of the system's direction.

A critical component necessary for a school leader's success is the on-going support provided by our Leadership Development staff and our Leader Mentors. Our newest school leaders are provided with one-on-one support, as well as training opportunities in group sessions through *Just-in-Time Training*. This training allows a newly appointed principal and/or assistant principal the opportunity to work with experienced leaders to develop an understanding of the school community and culture, achievement results, operations and processing, and school initiatives.

Representative Sessions for Principals
- FTE and Budget
- Monitoring and Updating the Local School Plan for Improvement
- Planning and Delivering Effective Staff Development
- Evaluating the Impact of Actions Taken to Improve Student Achievement
- Developing a Staffing Plan
- Selecting and Retaining Quality Personnel
- Persistently Successful Principals
- End-of-Year and Beginning-of-Year Procedures

Representative Sessions for Assistant Principals
- Goals for Teachers & Creating a Positive Learning Environment
- Benchmarks/Using Data
- Strategies for Supporting Teachers
- RTI Process
- Organizational Strategies
- Dealing with Difficult People

The Rainwater Charitable Foundation

Richard Rainwater established the Rainwater Charitable Foundation, based in Fort Worth, TX, to help children in the United States live a good life, specifically targeting those children who are born into poverty. His goal is to support educational programs with a demonstrated track record of success targeting programs that train and support school leaders, programs that prepare young children for success in elementary school and beyond, and programs that engage children in their schooling and develop in them a life-long passion for learning.

Richard Rainwater, a prominent investor, directs the funds from the Rainwater Charitable Foundation. He was the key figure in the formation of several major corporations, including Columbia/HCA Hospital Corporation, Crescent Real Estate Equities, and Pioneer Natural Resources. His love for children and his deep caring for families in difficult circumstances have inspired his commitment to positive solutions for children.